The Measurement of EMPLOYMENT and UNEMPLOYMENT by the BUREAU OF THE CENSUS in its CURRENT POPULATION SURVEY

Report of the
Special Advisory Committee
on Employment Statistics

August 1954

GREENWOOD PRESS, PUBLISHERS
WESTPORT, CONNECTICUT

Library of Congress Cataloging in Publication Data

United States. Dept. of Commerce. Special Advisory Committee on Employment Statistics.

The measurement of employment and unemployment by the Bureau of the Census in its current population survey.

Reprint of the 1954 ed. published by U.S. Dept. of Commerce, Special Advisory Committee on Employment Statistics.

1. Labor supply--United States--Statistical methods.
2. Unemployed--United States--Statistical methods.
I. Title.

[HD5711.U542 1979] 331.1'1'0973 78-11657

ISBN 0-313-20691-0

Originally published in 1954 by the Special Advisory Committee on Employment Statistics.

Reprinted in 1978 by Greenwood Press, Inc.,
51 Riverside Avenue, Westport, CT 06880

Printed in the United States of America

10 9 8 7 6 5 4 3 2 1

LETTER OF TRANSMITTAL

Special Advisory Committee
on Employment Statistics

August 16, 1954

The Honorable
The Secretary of Commerce

Dear Mr. Secretary:

We have the honor to submit to you herewith our report on the measurement of employment and unemployment by the Bureau of the Census in its Current Population Survey. Our inquiry has been one of modest scope. A larger group with greater resources should go to work on the unsolved problems and long-run questions that we have discussed in the report. While the Census methods and operations are sound fundamentally, they have been weakened by a lack of funds adequate for the tasks that were attempted. They need reinforcement and improvement so that they may produce estimates that will be satisfactory for the important public uses they can serve.

We commend to you the Director of the Bureau of the Census and the members of his staff for the wholehearted cooperation they have given us in our work and for their forward looking attitude toward the testing and improvements of their surveys.

The Committee had the benefit of advice from Dr. William G. Cochran of The Johns Hopkins University in its consideration of a number of statistical problems.

Respectfully submitted,

Frederick F. Stephan, Chairman
Lester R. Frankel
Lazare Teper

CONTENTS

NOTE.--The material comprising Appendixes 3 through 12 is issued as a separate part of this report and may be obtained upon request from the Bureau of the Census.

SPECIAL ADVISORY COMMITTEE ON EMPLOYMENT STATISTICS

Frederick F. Stephan, Chairman
Professor of Social Statistics, Princeton University

Lester R. Frankel
Vice President, Alfred Politz Research, Inc.

Lazare Teper
Director, Research Department, International Ladies' Garment Workers' Union

I. THE TASK OF THE COMMITTEE

This Committee was appointed by the Secretary of Commerce, on the advice of the Director of the Census, to investigate certain problems in the estimates of employment and unemployment that are obtained from the Bureau's monthly Current Population Survey. These problems arose in the following manner:

(1) For more than eleven years the Census Bureau has conducted a monthly survey of the population to estimate the number of persons who are employed, the number who are not employed but looking for work, and the number that are neither employed nor seeking work. These and a number of other classifications portray the activity of our population. Information thus obtained is classified according to age, sex, various broad classes of occupations and industries, hours of work, duration of unemployment, and other pertinent categories that help to describe people in and out of the labor force. In addition to information about the labor force, the Current Population Survey obtains information annually or at other times on the incomes of individuals and families and on other economic and demographic subjects. Information that is provided by these surveys is used not only to inform the public about the condition of the labor force but as one of the fundamental measures of economic conditions needed by the Federal Government.

(2) The Census Bureau's survey covers only a sample of the population. It would be prohibitively costly to canvass the whole population every month, and sufficiently accurate results can be obtained from a thorough coverage of a rigorously chosen sample. Until recently the Census Bureau has obtained the information on which the labor force estimates are based from the people who live in about

21,000 households* located in 68 areas. These areas are counties, or groups of adjacent counties, selected from all parts of the United States in a manner that seeks to represent every major region and type of community, in so far as that can be done with only this number of locations.

(3) The Census Bureau had considered some years ago the advantages that could be obtained by increasing the number of areas covered by the sample and a number of other technical improvements that could increase the accuracy and usefulness of the surveys including the possibility of obtaining reasonably reliable estimates for the principal regions of the United States. After more than a year of preparations and trials, the Census Bureau set in operation a new sample survey in which the same number of households that was included in the old survey is canvassed but they are located in 230 areas instead of 68. The first full-scale survey of the labor force based on this sample was made in January 1954. Meanwhile the old sample was also covered, since it was important to continue it until the new sample was fully established. In the selection of the 230 areas no account was taken of the 68 area sample, but the design provided that the major metropolitan areas would be represented, as had been the case in the 68 area design. In overlapping areas the same households were included in the sample.

(4) The January estimates based on the old sample were prepared and published at the usual time, early in February. The estimates based on the new sample were prepared immediately after the

---

* The sample consists of about 25,000 dwelling units or other living quarters, some of which are vacant or occupied by persons whose residence is elsewhere and therefore not to be enumerated at this address for the survey. In addition, between 500 and 1,000 households are not interviewed because their members are temporarily absent or not at home. Thus only about 21,000 households are actually enumerated each month.

regular estimates were finished. The two sets of estimates agreed quite closely on many items but there were major differences in the case of unemployment and certain other categories. For example, the number of persons 14 years of age or older that were estimated to be employed in the week of January 3 to 9, 1954 was:

	Employed	In agriculture	In non-agricultural industries
68 area survey ...	59,778,000	5,345,000	54,433,000
230 area survey...	59,753,000	5,284,000	54,469,000
Difference	25,000	61,000	36,000

but the number reported as unemployed was:

68 area survey ...	2,359,000
230 area survey ...	3,087,000
Difference	728,000

The discrepancy in the estimate of unemployment was particularly serious because it occurred in a period of rising unemployment and concern about the trend of business. It exceeded by a wide margin the extent to which two surveys of this type may usually be expected to differ.*

The staff of the Bureau of the Census started a number of studies of factors that could have contributed to the discrepancy.

The old survey was continued in February to obtain estimates for that month, and special steps were taken to remedy what appeared to have been a weakness in the operation of the survey resulting from

* In comparing the surveys, one should take account of the fact that about 27 percent of the households were common to both samples because they were located in areas which were included in both sample designs.

concentration of effort on the establishment of the new sample. In particular, conferences and refresher sessions were held with interviewers in both samples to make sure that the standard procedures and instructions were still being followed accurately.

The results of the new sample survey for January were published with a statement that the source of the differences was being investigated and an explanation of the causes would be published when they had been determined.

The Census Bureau was thus confronted by a number of problems: Was the new sample design defective? Was the new survey operated incorrectly? Was the old survey in error and if so, why and how much? Is the count of the "unemployed" inherently inaccurate? How much of the difference may be due to the vagaries of chance in the selection of the samples and how much to other causes?

To help in determining the answers to these questions and to assure the public that the review of the principles and the facts is not obscured by political considerations, the Secretary of Commerce and the Director of the Census asked the members of this Committee to review the results of the inquiries made by the staff, to suggest further studies, and to formulate recommendations for making the results of the Current Population Survey as useful as possible in indicating both the levels of employment and unemployment and the amount and direction of change. The letter of appointment is attached. (See Appendix 1.) In addition to this initial request, the Committee received assurances that it should not confine inquiries to the questions that were posed but should seek out the truth about the causes underlying the problems.

We appreciate deeply the opportunity we have had to discuss these questions with Assistant Secretary Lothair Teetor and the helpful interest he has shown in its work. The Director of the Census, Dr. Robert W. Burgess, and the members of his senior staff have been unstinting in their efforts to obtain for the Committee the information it needed. They have made great contributions to the work of the Committee in many ways.

The Committee has made one specific recommendation prior to this report. At its first regular meeting (following the initial discussions with members of the staff of the Bureau about various studies that were under way) the Committee received the results of the old and the new survey for February. These results showed discrepancies that were substantial but smaller than those that appeared in the January surveys. The Committee's inquiries brought to light the serious difficulties that resulted from the concurrent operation in the field of two surveys with a supervisory staff essentially carrying a double load. It was clear to the Committee, for reasons set forth more fully in the attached letter to the Director of the Census (See Appendix 2.) that the continuation of the old survey would strain the organization responsible for the field work and endanger the quality of both surveys. Accordingly, the Committee recommended that the 68 area survey not be extended into March.

For the most part, this report is a summary of information obtained in the course of a number of long conferences with the staff of the Census Bureau supplemented by material requested by mail and by a few conferences of individual Committee members with the Bureau's personnel in several field offices. The Committee has also reviewed much of the literature bearing directly on the survey of the labor force but has not attempted to incorporate or summarize it. Attached to this report, however, are two Census memoranda: "Statement on Decision to change to 230-area Design for CPS" (Appendix 4) and "Concepts and Methods Used in the Current Labor Force Statistics Prepared by the Bureau of the Census" (Appendix 5) which provide a description of the methodology used in these inquiries.

The task of the Committee did not include a full investigation of the field operations of the Current Population Survey or conferences with the many individuals who were interested in the problem. The Committee did not have the time or resources to undertake extensive analyses and checking operations of its own. It expected from the beginning to transmit in its report many problems that could not be solved but that merit intensive study by persons who are in a better position to pursue them.

The work of the Bureau of the Census has recently undergone a general review by the Intensive Review Committee under the chairmanship of Dr. Ralph J. Watkins. This review included a general evaluation of the Bureau's work in the field of the labor force. The report of one of its panels that was appointed specifically for this field is an excellent summary of the problems of labor force measurement. It is included in this report as Appendix 3. We are in general agreement with the analysis and recommendations reported by the panel and on this subject by the Intensive Review Committee.

Even if the report of the Intensive Review Committee were not available we could not undertake a general appraisal of the work of the Census Bureau in the field of the labor force, giving equal attention to the problems that have been solved and to those that have not. Our task is to investigate the problems raised by the January discrepancy, to propose studies to seek out the causes, and to recommend improvements.

While we are called upon primarily to be constructive critics and examiners, we must also point out that over the past decade a great part of the task of building up a sound monthly survey of the labor force, of developing the interviewing methods and classifications, of applying modern sampling methods, of measuring and reporting to the public the degree of sampling variation involved in the estimates, and of extending the usefulness of the results by providing detailed tabulations and supplementary information has been performed by the Census Bureau. It has attempted through experimentation and special studies to overcome serious technical problems that arose in the past. Its difficulties in the present instance stem in large measure from its attempt to make important improvements with funds and personnel insufficient to make the transition without much risk of trouble. In this as in previous problems it has had the advice and help of other agencies in planning the change of sample. If in the succeeding discussion the contributions and achievements of the Census Bureau appear to be overshadowed by the discrepancies and weaknesses, that is to be regretted. Relatively few surveys are put to a test such as this has had. There are many weaknesses in important sources of information, both public and private, that have not been brought to light, and any careful examination that revealed them would likewise tend to overshadow their merits. Nonetheless the discovery and remedy of defects is the only road toward more reliable and more useful information.

II. THE OPERATIONS OF THE MONTHLY CURRENT POPULATION SURVEY

The pursuit of the problems with which the Committee was concerned inevitably led it to a detailed examination of the survey procedure and the actual operations as well as the results they produced. In the first place it was necessary to consider specifically the various points at which the old and the new surveys differed. Until this was done there was always a possibility that some major cause of discrepancy had been overlooked.

Almost any part of the complex operation of conducting a nation-wide canvass could distort the estimates. For this reason the whole operation is performed by the Census Bureau according to elaborate procedures and by a staff that has had fairly standard training in them.

The work of preparing estimates of employment and unemployment can be described as a series of steps although some of them are taken infrequently and others simultaneously or repetitively. They do proceed, however, in a fairly logical order and a brief description of them will prepare the way for a step by step comparison of the old and the new surveys. They start with the decisions about what will be measured and end with the publication of estimates. These steps are:

1. Definition of employment, unemployment and other categories of economic activity according to which the population is counted;

2. The preparation of suitable questions designed to elicit, from the people interviewed, the information necessary to classify them as well as the other members of their households accurately into the various categories;

3. The determination of an efficient sampling procedure (complete enumerations of the population on a month-to-month basis are impossible, and for that matter unnecessary, because information with an adequate degree of approximation can be secured by partial enumerations for the kind of data that are needed currently);

4. The development of techniques for producing the final estimates on the basis of the information obtained by means of sampling;

5. The determination of the areas to be included in the sample and the households to be covered within them;

6. The development of appropriate instructions to the interviewers and other personnel, and selection, training and supervision of the field staff;

7. The taking of trial enumerations for the completion of the training of enumerators and for the purpose of testing out procedures;

8. The actual execution, on a monthly basis, of the regular field operation needed in the making of a survey, including inter-

viewing, follow-up, editing of schedules, transmission of the results to the central office;

9. Processing and tabulation of the data received from the field and computation of the detailed estimates;

10. Overall review of the data and of operating reports, development and application of procedures to ensure continued reliability of data, and integration of the estimates and related information collected by governmental agencies;

11. Preparation and issuance of press releases and detailed reports to the public.

The Committee has given some attention to each of the steps in the developments of the labor force estimates but has concentrated its attention on those issues which bear most on the accuracy of the survey results and the differences between the old and the new survey.*

III. SUMMARY OF GENERAL CONCLUSIONS

A number of particular conclusions and recommendations are presented in the next section "Committee Findings" in connection with the topics to which they apply. The following general conclusions emerge from our inquiries:

1. The discrepancy between the estimates derived from the old and new sample for January appears to have been due primarily to operating difficulties brought about by the transition and is there-

* Appendix 6 discusses some of the issues in the definition and classification of the labor force.

fore of a temporary nature. Nevertheless, it focussed attention on the fact that there are serious weaknesses in the labor force survey due to the inherent difficulty of some of the classifications that are attempted, the nature of the extended field operations that are necessary to cover the whole country, the limitations of funds and personnel available for the work, the unresolved technical problems that await research, and a variety of problems connected with interviewing.

2. The discrepancy was reduced substantially in the survey for February and there was no evidence to justify an alteration of the plans previously made for completing the transition from the 68 area sample to the new 230 area sample. No fundamental flaws were discovered in the new sample design or in the operating procedures of the new survey.

3. The Committee is of the opinion that the 230 area sample is an advance over the old design based on 68 areas and that it reflects changes in the labor force in a more sensitive manner than heretofore. However, the Committee feels that the new design needs to be strengthened further both through a further increase in the number of areas in the sample design and the use of a substantially larger number of households. At the same time, the Committee strongly urges that the use of controls and quality checks at all stages of enumeration be developed to the point where the essential accuracy of the information is assured.

4. The Committee believes that the old and the new sample data can be utilized as a consecutive series through a number of adjustment steps, the first of which has already been undertaken by the Census when it released its preliminary data for unemployment levels in connection with the March labor force statistics. This work needs to be continued in order to extend and refine these adjustments

5. Measures of the accuracy of the labor force data should be coupled more prominently with the monthly estimates both in the

releases to the press as well as in the more detailed final reports. They should include appropriate allowances for all the factors which bear on it. Tables of sampling errors have been published in the past but they should be extended to take account not only of the factors due to sampling but to all other major causes of inaccuracy as well. It should be made clear to the public that all measurement in this and many similar areas is approximate and that the determination of the accuracy to be attained is governed both by the needs for precision and by the amounts of funds that can be devoted to the survey.

6. Field procedures now in use need to be strengthened to achieve better performance and control of the processes of obtaining labor force information from the households in the sample. Specifically, there is need for closer contacts between supervisors and the interviewers working under them, further development of supervisory techniques and practices, the perfection of adequate control checks and qualitative evaluations of the work of individual interviewers as well as of summary results, research into the prevalent causes of errors throughout the survey operation, and development of more realistic performance standards for the work. Moreover, there is need to correct some of the adverse effects brought about by mechanization of operations and to discover still better ways for conducting routine processes of recording and tabulating of data obtained in the course of the field work. Careful attention should be given to the work load assigned to the interviewers, to their rate of pay, to recognition of superior performance and to a number of other aspects of field work which are important in the maintenance of high standards.

7. The Committee believes that the composite estimating procedure which has been introduced in the new sample has considerable merit and is apt to improve the accuracy of measurement for a number of labor force categories though unfortunately not for the estimates of unemployment at the present time. The Committee also believes that there are some potential hazards in this as well as alternative estimating procedures which should be investigated

thoroughly. Until adequate safeguards can be developed to protect against them, the estimating procedure should be regarded as experimental, and appropriate cautions should be included in the publications in which the estimates are released. Special attention should be given to the investigation of the differences between the results of the interviews with households which have just been introduced into the labor force sample and those obtained from the households which have been covered by the sample in the previous months, since these differences are the principal sources of uncertainty about the accuracy of the new procedure and also of alternative procedures.

8. The concepts of unemployment and other labor force categories that are used as the basis for the monthly surveys are in need of a general overhauling. They were developed, for the most part, during the depression years of the thirties and were at the time a very substantial improvement over the previously-utilized concepts. Nonetheless they still depend rather heavily upon personal evaluations by the respondents, and to some extent by the interviewers of attitudes towards labor force status rather than upon objective criteria.

Perfection cannot be expected in this field because of the continued existence of marginal situations which complicate classification, the practice of obtaining information about all members of a household through one of them, and the need for utilizing rigid lines of demarcation between the different groups in the population when in fact they may be more or less fluid. Nevertheless considerable improvement seems possible through additional experimentation with the concepts and questionnaires used in the interviewing and by other means.

Additional improvements can be made in the system of questioning which is used by interviewers to obtain the required information. Similarly, improvements can be made in the schedule forms of the questionnaires. These reviews and improvements should be undertaken, as in the past, in cooperation with other governmental agencies and should be facilitated by adequate budgetary provisions and by the increase in the specialized staff qualified in the field of labor market behavior.

9. The Current Population Survey has been operated under severe restrictions due to limitation and uncertainty of budgetary allocations. Budgetary problems, in part, have contributed to the difficulties which have arisen in the transition from the old to the new sample design. It is the hope of the Committee that Congress will be asked to provide and will provide sufficient funds to support the work needed to insure the maximum accuracy of the survey results on the basis of the present design and for subsequent strengthening of the sample in line with the Committee's recommendations.

10. The Committee is fully aware of the limited extent of its inquiry and believes that a larger and more representative committee with greater resources than those available to this Committee should be appointed to carry forward the study of this problem in cooperation with the Bureau of the Census. Such a committee, composed of persons both from within and without the government, should be broadly representative of the various groups concerned with the labor market analysis, including persons in professions, the administration of unemployment insurance and employment services, defense planning, business, labor and agriculture as well as economic and population research workers concerned with this area. The Committee should also include proper representation of persons who by their experience and competence are well qualified to contribute to the solution of the many technical and statistical problems in this field.

IV. COMMITTEE FINDINGS

More specifically, the Committee inquiry led to the following findings:

A. Similarities and Differences between the Old and the New Surveys

An examination of concepts and procedures used in conducting the old and the new sample surveys showed many similarities in procedures. Yet, there were a number of dissimilarities which throw some light on the discrepancies in the survey results. The points of similarity and difference between the two surveys are shown below:

a. The definitions of employment, unemployment and other labor force categories were identical in both surveys.

b. The questions used for enumeration purposes were also identical.

c. The sampling was similar in many respects but not in all. The geographic distribution of the samples differed. While the old sample was based on enumeration in 68 areas, the new sample gathered data in 230 areas. However 36 areas were included in whole or in part in both samples. In both cases completed interviews were obtained in approximately 21,000 households. The general statistical principles used in selection of the households to be included in each of the areas were substantially the same in both surveys.

   The effect of the selection of the sample areas can be considered separately from that of the selection of households within these areas. For example, labor force data for these areas as collected in the 1950 Census of Population can be deemed a sample for the estimation of the labor force at the time of that census.

The resulting estimates of both the old and the new sample show relatively small differences in comparison with the actual count obtained by the Census (See Appendix 10 for the statistical data). In addition, it is possible to calculate with some accuracy the amount of variation which is introduced into the labor force estimates by the selection of 68 or the 230 areas apart from the effect of sampling households within an area and other influences. Both the direct comparison afforded by Appendix 10 and the estimates of sampling variation make it reasonably clear that no more than a small fraction of the discrepancy between the results of the old and the new survey figures in January can be attributed to the choice of sample areas.

The selection of the sample of households within the sample areas introduces another element of sampling variation. Here again it is possible to estimate the magnitude of this source of variation from the data provided by the Current Population Survey itself. The combined effect of taking a sample of areas and taking a sample of households within each of them makes it appear improbable that as much as one half of the January unemployment discrepancy is due to these two sources. It is likely that a much smaller fraction can be attributed to them, and that the greater part of the discrepancy is to be accounted for by other factors.

d. Both surveys use the same method of discontinuing one fourth of the dwelling units in the sample each month and replacing them with an equivalent number of dwelling units drawn from the same sampling areas. Thus the dwelling units in the sample are rotated from month to month and households do not remain in the sample indefinitely. The counties in the sample are not changed. A detailed explanation of the system of replacement and rotation is given in Appendix 5, page A-26. The rotation introduces a problem concerning the interviewing and responses of the households as they enter the sample and proceed to successive monthly inquiries about their members' participation in the labor force. It has been observed in the 68 area sample, and to some extent in the 230 area sample, that for reasons as yet unexplained the rate of unemployment of the members of households that were brought into the sample in the same month (referred to as a rotation group) usually is higher for the rotation group that is being interviewed for the first time than it is for the rotation groups that were interviewed in the preceding month. Yet each of the rotation groups is a comparable and proper sample in its own right. It is not known whether this difference is a matter of over-reporting unemployment in the first month or under-reporting in the next three months following the introduction of the group of households into the sample. It may be both. Moreover, because the proportion of newly introduced households was higher in the 230 area survey at the time it was completed in January than it was in the 68 area survey, this tendency of the newest rotation group to show a higher rate of unemployment may account for some of the differences in the estimates provided by the two surveys. The staff of the Census Bureau has estimated the difference that this tendency may have produced at about 70,000 unemployed persons. Appendix 12 discusses some of the problems of determining the magnitude of this tendency and its effect on the estimation procedures.

e. The old survey was conducted predominantly by an experienced field staff. The new survey, with the exception of those areas that are common to both samples, was conducted in the main with new enumerators. No differences were found in the instructions and procedures that the interviewers were to follow that could have made a major contribution to the discrepancy.

f. The activation of the new survey created a number of problems of training and supervision which had different effects on the two surveys. The new enumerators had to be selected and trained during the last three or four months of 1953. A considerable amount of special field work had to be done for the selection of the new sample. The new survey had to be put through a series of trial enumerations. They began with a dry-run in 6 sample areas in one section of the country, taken in September and October 1953. They continued with a trial survey in 70 areas in November, expanded to 142 areas in December. The full 230 areas were covered for the first time in January 1954. The supervisory staff, which had been curtailed since the middle of 1953 had to handle both surveys with limited additional assistance from staff detailed from Washington. While the supervisory staff was occupied with additional assignments such as the development of the list of households to be enumerated and in the selection and training of new personnel and other duties, they were instructed to suspend almost all review sessions and meetings with the old interviewers beginning with September 1953. During the entire period of initiating the new sample the supervision and supplemental training of the experienced interviewers on the 68 area survey were conducted almost entirely by mail, leaving interviewers who had previously been accustomed to a greater degree of personal supervision free to proceed on their own. Apparently this resulted in a deterioration of performance. The effect was particularly marked on the estimate of unemployment which is normally difficult to measure.

g. After it was found that the unemployment estimates for January differed by more than could be accounted for by the change in the samples, provision was made for special training of interviewers in both the 68 area and 230 area surveys prior to the February canvass. Because of this and perhaps other factors the estimates for February were considerably closer together and the differences for that month might well have been due to sampling variation. However, evidence available from very limited rechecks on interviews in the February survey suggests that some of the differences due to interviewing still persisted. In any event, these results suggest that at least half or perhaps considerably more of the difference in January occurred from causes other than the change in samples, and that the principal source of the nonsampling part of the discrepancy was the suspension of personal supervisory contact for the extended period involved in making the changeover.

h. The same estimating technique was used for both surveys in the preparation of January 1954 estimates. A different estimating technique has been introduced in the new sample beginning with February 1954; it is discussed later in the report.

i. In January both surveys obtained information about labor force characteristics for the same week of the month. However, the actual enumeration, which started in the succeeding week, extended over nearly two weeks in the case of the new sample as compared with approximately one week in the case of the old sample. Only 85 percent of the new sample had been interviewed in the first week of enumeration in January compared with 98 percent of the old sample. This may have had some effect on the accuracy of the estimates through the dimming of recollections of respondents regarding events in the survey week. In March when the new sample was operating alone, the enumerators appeared to be completing the same percentage of their interviews in the first week as they had in the old sample.

j. In January 1954, a larger proportion of interviews were conducted by telephone in the case of the old sample than in the case of the new sample. Studies made at the time telephone interviewing was introduced in 1951 and 1952 indicate that the quality of telephone and personal interviews was probably about the same for estimating labor force characteristics at that time. These tests were conducted, however, during the comparative stability of the labor market at a time when unemployment was relatively low. In a period when unemployment is on the increase, the tests might have produced different results in view of the greater number of marginal situations for which adequate information must be obtained. Another evaluation of this procedure is greatly needed.

k. There were no substantive changes in the tabulating procedures in the case of data gathered from the new sample.

l. In summary, therefore, the examination of the two surveys revealed that they relied on the same conceptual definitions and on similar methodological principles. While most estimates agreed well, there was a significant difference in the unemployment estimates for January, a difference about twice as large as the most extreme difference that should have been expected from the use of samples in place of a full scale census. It appears that at least half and perhaps much more of the total difference arose because of differences in the interviewing, for the most part as a result of inadequate supervision in the old sample areas during the period of shifting samples. Steps taken to improve training in the 68 area sample prior to the February survey, helped to reduce materially the discrepancies between this and the 230 area survey. No further comparison could be made since the 68 area survey was discontinued in March.

B. Comparative Accuracy of the Two Surveys

The two surveys have been compared with each other and with information derived from the 1940 and 1950 censuses of population, the reports of unemployment insurance claims, and with other data in order to throw light on the nature of the discrepancies. In addition, comparisons were made between detailed tabulations in order to localize the differences, if possible. While the discrepancies were not evenly spread through these tabulations, they were not concentrated, on the other hand, in a way which revealed striking or fundamental differences in detail between the two surveys.

a. The comparisons with census data for 1940 and 1950 give evidence that the first stage of sampling, i.e., the selection of geographic areas within which people were to be interviewed, yields somewhat more accurate results for the new survey than for the old one. It is only a partial test since it did not include the effect of sampling households within each of the 230 areas or the effect of any differences in the quality of interviewing. This result, of course, was consistent with the principles of sampling on which the change from 68 to 230 areas was predicated.

b. The new survey appeared to be more accurate than the old one on the basis of a comparison between the estimates of population by age and sex that could be derived from it and the more accurate independent population projections that are based on previous censuses.

c. At various other points internal evidence suggests that the quality of the interviewing for the new survey was superior to that of the old during the changeover period.

d. The inclusion of 230 areas in the sample is a distinct advance over the inclusion of only 68 areas in the sample selected 10 years earlier. In addition, the improvement in accuracy that was attained by use of demographic and economic data in the original establishment of the 68 area sample has weakened with the passage of time.

c. The estimates based on the old sample from September 1953 through January 1954 seemed to show increasing disparities when compared with the corresponding unemployment insurance claim statistics. This suggests that the estimates may have been deteriorating. On the other hand, the higher unemployment figures for January based on the new sample seemed more nearly consistent with the unemployment insurance data.

f. From these considerations and other evidence, the Committee believes that on the basis of the concepts used by the Census Bureau in defining employment, unemployment and other characteristics of the labor force, the new sample estimates are the more accurate and should be used in preference to the old survey estimates to represent the economic status of the population in

January 1954. This is not to imply that there were no sources of inaccuracy in the 230 area sample estimate such as those that might be expected to result from the comparatively limited experience of the new interviewers and the insufficient opportunity to complete the discovery and elimination of principal sources of error in the process of enumeration. The new interviewers, fresh from training and with assurance of future work before them may have succeeded in doing a more adequate job than they will in the future months. The possibility of deterioration in their performance should not be overlooked.* It may arise under the presently contemplated practices of supervision which provide less frequent personal contact with the supervisor and the greater reliance on written instructions as a basis for renewing and maintaining competence in the use of complicated rules and procedures, as well as the usual skills of good enumerators.

C. Adequacy of the Sample Size

When it is granted that the accuracy of the new sample is greater than that of the old one, the question still remains of determining whether the estimates as compiled on the basis of interviews in about 21,000 households provide information with a degree of accuracy sufficient for most public purposes. Some of the tests which have been made by comparing national totals for the 1950 census with estimates derived from the complete counts in the 230 areas in the same census raise doubts in the minds of the Committee regarding the adequacy of the new sample for the making of regional estimates, except possibly for a few of the larger labor force groupings. Similarly, doubts exist with regard to the adequacy of the sample for national estimates of the small subdivisions of the labor force. Finally, the most

* The absence of the expected rise in the labor force in June 1954 when students and new graduates usually enter the labor market pinpoints this observation. Careful analyses of these figures should be made to make sure that the results were not due to deterioration of interviewer performance.

important of all, neither the old nor the new sample is of adequate size to assure measures of unemployment and other characteristics as accurate as may be needed for many public purposes. For these reasons the Committee believes a substantially larger sample is needed both to cover more areas and to increase the number of households in each. The larger sample in individual areas would tend to reduce the effect of unwitting errors committed by a small number of enumerators and to facilitate studies of the consistency of interviewers' performance in order to insure a greater control of the quality of the work.

The Committee has observed in the press and elsewhere many comments that reveal that there is an insufficient understanding of the nature of enumerations and the degree of precision which they can attain. This is especially true of sample enumerations. Scientists know well that all measurements are at best approximate. The degree of approximation can frequently be estimated from the survey data by dependable statistical techniques. However, the results of measurement are only too frequently treated as though they are exactly true. For example, the March survey of the labor force reported an estimate of unemployment that was but 54,000 greater than that shown in February. This result was reported by the Census as "practically the same" because it was well within the limit of the month-to-month variation in the survey results that must be expected solely due to chance. However, it was cited in the press as though it were an accurate measure of the direction and amount of change.

The tendency of the public and press to ignore the degree of approximation is reinforced by the practice followed by the Census of releasing estimates carried out to the nearest 1,000 and also by the practice of publishing estimates of sampling error in relatively obscure portions of the report and nowhere in the press releases. Since an appropriate degree of caution must be exercised in using statistical data, it is important to indicate at all times the extent of precision with which they are compiled and make the user aware of the degree of approximation taken into account. To accomplish this, estimates of sampling errors should be computed from current data because the sampling errors not only change with the level of a particular category within the labor force but also with the nature of its distribution in the population. Estimates of sampling error include only part of the errors which originate in the process of interviewing, either due to inaccuracies of response or defects of interviewing. It is important that estimates of the magnitude of inaccuracy due to causes other than sampling should be provided in addition to the usual estimates of sampling error.

D. Questionnaire and Interview*

A review of the questionnaire and the interviewing situation led the Committee to question the extent to which the efforts to economize and to mechanize processing of interview results possibly increased errors on the part of the interviewing staff. For example, the questionnaire has been compressed on a comparatively small card, using unduly small print and an arrangement not always easy to follow. Furthermore, some of the questions provided by the schedule presume that satisfactory responses would be given in the first instance by the respondents. Any evidence to the contrary which arises in the course of the interview creates special problems of recording, which may result in some conflicts between the different sections of the questionnaires and force interviewers to make on-the-spot decisions which should preferably be resolved by the central office personnel. The questionnaire is intended to provide a systematic record of the facts for a large proportion of all interviews. However, many interviews reveal more complex situations to handle which the interviewers must remember and apply certain specific rules. In these instances they must use their own ingenuity rather than a printed pattern of questioning to obtain accurate data. There is a danger in these cases that they may make their decisions in a biased and inappropriate manner especially if their supervisors are not aware of the problems that arise in each interview and how the interviewers are resolving them. This is one of the reasons why adequate supervision and con-

---

* See Appendix 7 for an additional discussion of the problems of the interview and questionnaire.

stant coaching of interviewers is a paramount necessity in the over-all operation and why the manual of instructions to interviewers tends to become unduly voluminous and complex. The Committee is of the opinion that much research needs to be undertaken to determine how to revise the questionnaire so that it will permit the collection of necessary information with a minimum of personal interpretations on the part of the interviewer.

At all times, but particularly when a sample is as widely spread as it is in the new design, it is important to insure the continued good quality of the responses obtained by the interviewers from the persons who furnish information about their households. This calls for a central checking operation designed to maintain quality standards and to insure that the performance of the individual interviewers remains on a high level. It may well be done by instituting a central or independent interviewing section, which would check the results of field enumerations on a systematic basis as well as follow-up by mail designed for the same purpose.

E. Control and Quality Check*

The principal checks on the performance of individual interviewers under the old sample included (a) checks on the comprehension of concepts, definitions, and procedures on the part of interviewers through group discussions, mock interviews, test exercises, etc., (b) analyses of time spent in interviewing and of the ratio of errors detected in the editing of completed schedules, (c) observations made by supervisors in their contacts with interviewers, and (d) a follow-up interview by the supervisors which was utilized in a small number of cases covered in the survey to check the completeness of coverage of households and persons in the subsampled segments. In addition, the supervisor accompanied new interviewers on trial interviews, accompanied other interviewers whom he regarded as weak for pur-

* See Appendix 8 for an additional discussion of these problems.

poses of observing their methods and helping clarify and improve their work, and reinterviewed the work of some of the interviewers as a method of evaluating the quality of their work.

When the plans were drawn for the new sample, it was considered necessary by the Census Bureau to make more formal quality control operations an integral part of the data collection program. As of this date, the following steps appear to have been taken:

a. The old sample controls of the performance of individual interviewers in terms of time taken in completing their assignments, the proportion of assigned households actually interviewed, the reasons for noninterviews, the extent of omissions, and analysis of such errors as are detectable in the course of a standard editing process continue to be maintained for the new sample.

b. A mail follow-up of interviewing for a modest number of households interviewed by each enumerator during a given month is being tested to provide a partial basis for a quality control system.

c. About two percent of households interviewed in the course of a month are revisited by district office personnel for a recheck interview, the results of which are thereafter compared and reconciled with the original information to determine the extent and character of possible discrepancies. This recheck also includes a check on coverage of households and persons.

The controls on efficient use of time, coverage of assigned household and errors detectable in editing appear to be valuable in obtaining a higher level of quality in the survey but their effect is rather definitely limited to checking the completeness of canvassing the sample and to detecting rather obvious errors affecting the accuracy of the information obtained in the course of the interviews. The extent to which editing can detect inaccuracies is limited since the schedule does not include all the detailed responses which the respondent gave to the interviewer but contains coded classifications based on those responses. Furthermore, the pressure brought to bear on interviewers through these controls and the instruction that the interviewers should pre-edit the questionnaire before sending them to the district office may tend to produce corrections that insure the internal consistency of the responses without necessarily insuring their accuracy. The emphasis on the time taken for the interviewing process and the attempt to spur on competition among interviewers in this regard by giving them the record of the performance of other interviewers as well as their own, may have an undesirable effect of sacrificing quality to speed in the interview process.

The mail follow-up may be a useful part of the program of control but its real utility as a quality test remains to be established. Some of the answers that are obtained on the mail questionnaires seem to be much less accurate than those obtained by direct interviewing. The mail follow-up suffers from the lapse of memory of many respondents and also because a substantial proportion of respondents fail to return the questionnaire. With all its defects, the mail questionnaire nevertheless offers an inexpensive check of several parts of survey performance.

The recheck interviewing of a random subsample of about two percent of the households appears to be a promising method for testing the average quality of the original interviews and for providing information for use in controlling quality. However, this method does not bring to light inaccuracies which are likely to be introduced by both the original interview and the recheck interview in the same households. Because of its cost it tends to be limited to much too small a part of the total sample. For most items in the enumeration reliable results may not be obtained until the recheck interviews have been accumulated over a considerable period of time. For such items then this recheck will be a rather sluggish indicator of the sources of inaccuracy that need correction. Even when this method does reveal specific types of discrepancies it will not necessarily indicate the particular nature of the errors or the ways in which they should be corrected. In spite of these limitations, the recheck interviews are being used to identify interviewers doing unsatisfactory work and corrective steps are currently being taken.

It should be recognized that a considerable degree of control of quality is achieved through the initial training, retraining, and supervision of interviewers. Even so, this type of control and the other types of controls previously described are not sufficient, in the opinion of the Committee, to achieve and maintain an adequate degree of accuracy in the information about unemployment and some of the other labor force categories. Additional means of controlling quality are needed.

F. Editing, Coding, and Tabulation Processes

The procedures for editing, coding and tabulating the household schedules received from the field have not been reviewed by this Committee and are not likely, in its opinion, to have been responsible for any substantial part of the discrepancies between the old and the new sample results. The only apparent innovation in this area was the use over the last several months of the Univac, an electronic computer, for the purpose of tabulating and computing the final estimates. One advantage of this process is in that it enables the Census to make current computations of sampling variation, a process which was time-consuming and costly under the previous methods. There are other important advantages in such processing but the Committee has not studied them or any disadvantages that may have been found during the first few months of operation. The possibilities of exploiting the capabilities of the computer should be explored in connection with the improvement of the existing questionnaires and even the review of the concepts since the new equipment makes feasible a number of more detailed or complex approaches that have not previously been feasible. Such matters as this are a proper subject for future investigation by a review committee as well as by the Census staff.

G. Estimating Procedure

Beginning with the estimates for February 1954 the Census Bureau has employed a new estimating procedure. It aims at an increase in accuracy by combining in an appropriate manner the results of two separate methods of estimating.

The first method is essentially the same as the procedure used in the preparation of estimates from the old 68 area sample. It starts with estimates of the population of the United States that are based on the 1950 Census and adjusted for changes that have taken place between 1950 and the current date. These adjustments can be readily made because the registration of births and deaths provides information about additions to the population and losses. Movements of people into and out of the United States are also readily measured. The increase in the ages of the population is easy to compute. Consequently, without any surveys, the number of people of a given sex and color in each age group is computed by the Census each year. The Current Population Survey is then used to prepare the estimates, in effect by computing, for each of the sex-color-age groups, the percentage of people found in each labor force classification, for the week for which the estimates are being prepared. This percentage is applied to the corresponding estimate of the number of people in the sex-color-age group and the resulting figure is the estimate for that group of the number of persons in the classification. Thus, if in the households covered by the survey the percentage of white men between 35 and 45 years of age who were unemployed in the second week of a certain month was 3.172 and the independent estimate of the number of men in this group was 9,427,000, the estimate of the number of unemployed men in this group is 3.172 percent of 9,427,000 or 299,000. This process is referred to as inflating the sample to national totals. The estimates for each of the sex-color-age groups are then combined to obtain various total figures for the final reports. The use of the independent estimates of the population makes these totals more accurate than estimates based only on the sample survey.

The second method of estimating is based on the changes that were recorded for those households in dwelling units that were included in both the survey of the preceding month and that of the current month. The information obtained for these persons, who constitute about three-fourths of the sample in the current month (when inflated to the national estimate in each month, as described for the first estimate) provides an estimate of the change in the number of persons in each of the labor force classifications. This estimated change is added to the estimate of the number in the classification in the preceding month to obtain an estimate for the current month.

Each pair of corresponding estimates made by the two methods is then averaged to form a final composite estimate. Analyses that were made prior to the adoption of the composite estimating procedure indicated that it would yield estimates of somewhat greater accuracy than the previous method, particularly for the measurement of month-to-month change, for most of the items that are reported. However, for the estimation of unemployment, little or no gain is expected from the new procedure and there may even be a slight loss of accuracy. There has not yet been sufficient time to test the extent of improvement achieved by the composite method.

The two estimating procedures will have the same average value over a period of time provided that, on the average, there are no differences in the measures obtained from the rotation groups that are in the sample for the first time from those in the sample a second, third, or fourth month, etc. However, for unemployment, there is evidence that such differences have existed and perhaps, also, smaller differences for certain other items. Because of these differences it turns out that if the new estimation procedure is applied to the survey results for the past six years the average of the estimates of unemployment would be somewhat lower than for the old, but estimates for other items would differ little, if any, on the average from the estimates derived previously.

Whether the new or old estimating procedure tends to be closer to the true value implied by the concept being measured cannot be established without further research since it is not clear whether the households interviewed for the first time or those which have been interviewed in preceding months provide information which is closer to reality.

Until this research is completed and the effects of repeated interviewing of the same households is determined, there will be a serious question about the accuracy of the estimates of unemployment by any estimating procedure. It is possible, of course, that the margin of uncertainty that is introduced by these effects may be less important than some other sources of uncertainty. For example, it may well be within the zone of uncertainty that results from sampling variation. It may be less important than certain problems of defining what kinds of persons are to be included in a classification such as that of the unemployed. It may even be eliminated by improvements in the field operations, without any direct effort to measure and correct the effects of repeated interviewing. However, the results of the first six months operation of the new sample suggest that the effects are not negligible. Consequently the Committee believes that the new composite method of estimation should be treated as an experimental procedure and should be used with appropriate safeguards to indicate each month whether it has produced results that may have been affected to an unusual degree by the differences encountered in repeated interviewing. There should also be a systematic study of its behavior under conditions different from those of the past few years.

H. Adjustment and Use of Past Series

The finding of the Committee that a large part of the discrepancy in estimates of unemployment for January 1954 was due to the deterioration of the field work performance in the collection of data for the 68 area sample, immediately raises a question about the accuracy of the results obtained from this sample in the preceding months. A comparison of the labor force figures for the last several years with certain other series of data clearly supports the view that the distortion began gradually around September 1953. This was the time at which the efforts of the supervisors began to be diverted to the work connected with the preparation of the new sample. An adjustment of the figures from that time on should be made in the light of all the important information which can be brought to bear on the problem of improving the accuracy of the estimates. It is too much to hope, however, for more than a crude adjustment and partial correction of the discrepancy.

To meet the immediate need for adjusted figures that offer a reasonably dependable link with the new estimates, the Census Bureau prepared a set of tentative adjustments in the unemployment estimates and published them with the concurrence of the Committee in the Monthly Report on the Labor Force for March 1954. The adjustments are based on the assumption of a progressive deterioration and the revised figures were obtained by applying a series of percentage adjustments that increase uniformly from 6 percent for September 1953 to 31 percent for January 1954. The latter figure is derived from the ratio of the estimate from the 230 area sample to that of the 68 area sample. These adjustments may be improved some months hence after additional study but for the time being they should serve immediate practical purposes of providing a continuous series.

I. Work Load

The accuracy of the results obtained under any survey procedure depends directly on the time and effort that the interviewers and that other staff members devote to carrying out the procedures. Unless at least a reasonable minimum of time is permitted for each step in the survey, a satisfactory degree of performance can hardly be expected. This is where pressure for greater economy and efficiency may defeat its own purpose unless adequate steps are taken simultaneously to maintain the quality of the work. After whatever slack there may have been in previous operations has been taken up, continued pressure tends to impel survey personnel to cut corners, to slight some of the necessary steps, to relax their vigilance in discovering errors and to omit steps that would prevent their occurrence. While the Committee did not make a thorough study of this phase of the Current Population Survey, it did find some evidence that suggests that relatively rigid production requirements or quotas were being employed in a way that tends to weaken the performance of the interviewers and lower the quality of the information that was obtained in the field.

The effects of this pressure are difficult to trace but it is obvious to any one who reads through the instruction book issued to the interviewers that there are many finer points and distinctions that are important to the accuracy of the estimates but which are not likely to be observed if the pressure for high production rates leaves too little time for further questioning and checking the instructions. There is an ever present danger that the emphasis on conformity by the questionnaires to specified patterns of accurate response may have an adverse effect on accuracy. The interviewers may actually be encouraged to introduce artificial consistency. The manual and the periodic instructions urge individual interviewers to edit their own returns before sending them to the central offices. Mistaken editing practices may easily escape detection thus endangering the quality of the results.

A further and more subtle effect of pressure is to exert a selective influence in the hiring, training and turnover of interviewers. Individuals who are uniformly conscientious about all the phases of the work that require care will be less likely to be hired and retained than interviewers who habitually meet only the minimum requirements of quality and put primary emphasis on "turning out the work." The editorial practice of judging individual interviewer performance first in terms of the number of inconsistencies or omitted questions and second in terms of the average time consumed in the interviewing process places too much emphasis on the mechanical rather than the qualitative features of the performance.

There is of course a maximum time that can be allotted for the work. It varies from place to place, depending on the interviewing conditions and even from one time of the year to another. Similarly, individual interviewers are to be expected to take somewhat different amounts of time in performing identical tasks. It appears, however, that there well may be an insufficient recognition of the differences in time due to such factors as well as the differences in the questionnaires themselves from one interviewing period to another.

When the employment situation changes, there may be many special conditions that require longer interviews to obtain the essential facts about each member of a household. For example, at certain times there may be more temporary lay-offs, more part-time work, greater confusion in the line of demarcation between being in or out of the labor force, and greater difficulty in determining the number of hours worked. Effective use of the present form of the questionnaire requires probing beyond the questions indicated on the form to get all the facts needed for proper classification. The neglect of some of the additional questions which are essential for accurate classification, may lead to substantial overstatement of full-time employment, since many individuals, when questioned, confuse the reporting of the normal hours of employment with those of the actual hours worked in a given survey period. Thus, it is necessary to ask a further question to verify the answer whenever the respondent reports, for example, 40 hours of work--the most likely rate for this kind of error. The lack of specific provision for such further inquiry and pressure on the interviewer to save time by merely recording the first answer he receives will tend toward overstatement of the actual number of hours worked for many individuals. Similarly, the questions relating to "looking for work," having a job but not being at work or being unable to work frequently require further questioning if the final classification is to be accurate. Interviewers who are working under pressure may well omit these inquiries and yet produce complete questionnaires that bear the marks of internal consistency. Some of these problems have been mentioned above in the sections on Control and Quality Check and Questionnaire and Interview.

The Committee believes, therefore, that the Census Bureau, and the review committee which is recommended below, should reexamine the present system of quota assignments to individual interviewers and give greater recognition than at the present to the qualitative factors which may affect the interview process.

Supplementary questions are often added to the Current Population Survey. Many of them are properly designed to obtain information on several aspects of the labor force behavior that need not be collected at monthly intervals. Others provide useful demographic or economic information about the changing patterns of the population as a whole. They serve an indirect purpose by varying the information sought by the survey and thus relieving the monotony of the standard questions for both the enumerators and the respondents. There is, of course, an ever-present danger that the supplementary questions may require an expenditure of time on the part of the interviewers beyond the limit of what they can give without adverse effects on the basic questionnaire. This, of course, may be avoided when appropriate allocation is made of additional time for the interviewing. In any case it is desirable that the supplementary inquiries be limited to subject matter for which adequate information is normally in possession of the respondents and which is appropriate to a survey devoted to the labor force.

The Committee notes that the Census Bureau should at all times operate the Current Population Survey with the full realization of the great importance to the nation of measures of labor force, employment and unemployment, and should avoid any contracts for service work for other agencies which are likely to impair the reliability of the CPS returns. Specifically, the Committee believes that, while the objective of doing appropriate jobs for other agencies is highly commendable, all such work should pay for the additional costs involved and should contribute a reasonable amount toward overhead and other costs. Furthermore, the supplements should be in the public interest, and should be sufficiently closely related to the other work of the Bureau to insure that they will not impair public acceptance of them as within the Bureau's proper functions or public confidence in other Census work.

J. Recommendations for Study by a Continuing Committee

Throughout the pages of this report there are a number of difficult problems that were beyond the powers of the Committee and the staff of the Bureau of the Census to solve in the time available to them. Some of them will require analysis of changes in the labor force and the operation of the labor force survey over a relatively long period of time and under conditions that are quite different from those that have prevailed during and since World War II. Preparations should be made for the collection of information for such studies when sudden changes take place in the labor market.

The degree of detail in the estimates, the classifications for which estimates should be prepared, and the degree of accuracy to be specified for each should be determined by a more searching study of the uses to which the labor force survey is and can be put. The appropriateness of the present definitions should be reviewed thoroughly, particularly in the case of the category of unemployment.

These are matters that should not be worked out by a single agency nor indeed by the Federal Government alone. The experience, judgment, and technical skill of persons who are specially concerned about the labor force in state agencies, business and industrial organizations, labor organizations and universities should be brought to bear on the problems. Greater time and resources than this Committee could devote to them are required. Because of the great importance of the labor force information and the nature of the work to be done, we recommend that a committee or commission of substantial stature be organized to conduct a program of studies and conferences leading to the solution of the major problems that are now revealed both by the progress that has been made and the discrepancies that have appeared in labor force measurement. Such a group, properly staffed and working closely with the Census Bureau and other interested government agencies, will be in a position to make a major contribution to the improvement of the measurement of the labor force.

Lester R. Frankel

Lazare Teper

Frederick F. Stephan
Chairman

The Measurement of
EMPLOYMENT and UNEMPLOYMENT
by the BUREAU OF THE CENSUS
in its CURRENT POPULATION SURVEY

APPENDIXES and BIBLIOGRAPHY

to the

Report of the
Special Advisory Committee
on Employment Statistics

August 1954

SPECIAL ADVISORY COMMITTEE ON EMPLOYMENT STATISTICS

Frederick F. Stephan, Chairman
Professor of Social Statistics, Princeton University

Lester R. Frankel
Vice President, Alfred Politz Research, Inc.

Lazare Teper
Director, Research Department, International Ladies' Garment Workers' Union

CONTENTS

APPENDIX 1

Letter of Appointment

February 23, 1954

Mr. Frederick F. Stephan
Department of Economics and Social Institutions
Princeton University
Box 337
Princeton, New Jersey

Dear Mr. Stephan:

In the process of introducing a revised sample based on 230 primary sampling units rather than 68 units for its Current Population Survey, the Bureau of the Census has run into certain problems on which we should appreciate some assistance from you.

The point is that some of the results of the first complete enumeration taken in January using the new sample differ from the results based on the old sample by substantially more than the range of variation expected from sampling theory. Comparisons to the two sets of results show close agreement on total volume of employment, but disagreement on some of the categories of employment, notably employment for 35 hours or more per week, and on unemployment. A matter of special concern is the figure for unemployment, 3,087,000 according to the new sample, as compared with 2,359,000 according to the old sample.

The experts of the Census Bureau are examining possible explanations of these differences. It is recognized that the differences may arise in part from sampling variation, and in part from differences in interview procedures, arising perhaps from differences in experience and training of enumerators. In connection with the February canvass now under way for both the old and new sample, the Field Division provided "refresher" training for interviewers and will conduct some check reinterviews. The experts are also summarizing the January results by various categories and developing measures of between-county variability by the use of the approximately comparable statistics of unemployment compensation claims for the sets of counties in the two samples.

To assist in examining this situation and to assure the public that the review of the principles and the facts is not obscured by political considerations, the Secretary of Commerce has authorized the forming of a special Advisory Committee to review the Census Bureau's analysis, to make such additional suggestions for studies of the immediate problem as it may wish, and to formulate recommendations for making

Mr. Frederick F. Stephan
February 23, 1954

the results from the Current Population Survey as useful as possible in indicating both the levels of employment and unemployment and the amount and direction of change. If the Committee believes that one cause of difficulty in using the figures is that users tend to expect a single figure to tell the whole story rather than to take into account also a group of related figures, its recommendations might include some comments along that line. The Committee will be free, of course, if it wishes, to note the need for a broad review of employment statistics in general including re-examination of the concepts of unemployment and applicability of sampling principles in this area. It is hoped that you will consent to serve as chairman of this committee with the expectation that you will have suggestions as to other members and as to the method of operation of the committee.

To meet the immediate problem, it will be helpful for you as chairman, with such other committee members as can be assembled, to spend a day at the earliest possible opportunity to review what has been done to date. A meeting of the entire committee should be held during the period March 3-6, when some results of the February canvass will become available. One or more additional meetings will probably be needed in the following week or several weeks.

Sincerely yours,

/s/

Robert W. Burgess
Director
Bureau of the Census

APPENDIX 2

Letter to Director on Continuation of 68-Area Sample Survey

March 6, 1954

Dr. Robert W. Burgess, Director
Bureau of the Census
Washington 25, D. C.

Dear Dr. Burgess:

We wish to transmit to you at this time the views of the Special Advisory Committee on Employment Statistics with respect to the continuation of the 68-area sample survey of the labor force. We have today received the results of the February survey and made a preliminary examination of them in relation to the results of the new 230-area sample survey. Prior to our meeting today we made a similar study of the results obtained in January and preceding months. Our study of the information up to this point convinces us no substantial contribution to the estimation of employment and unemployment can be expected from a repetition of the 68-area sample survey this month.

The considerations that lead us to this opinion include the following:

1. The information obtained in January and February has thrown considerable light on the nature of the differences between the two surveys.

2. Information we have received about the methods of operating the sample surveys make it clear that continued operation of the 68-area sample survey would weaken the new 230-area sample survey because much of the personnel and particularly the specially trained supervisors would be compelled to continue to carry a double load of work. The consequence might well be serious for both surveys.

3. The information we have received also convinces us that it is not feasible to maintain for another month the sample coverage and quality of interviewing in the 68-area sample survey that would be necessary to make it comparable with the normal operations of this survey. The reasons for this are many, including

Robert W. Burgess
March 6, 1954

> difficulties in the replacement of the households which have completed their period of participation in the survey and keeping together the interviewing staff in those areas that are not to be continued in the new survey.

We are continuing our examination of the information obtained from both surveys and the other information that you have provided concerning the methods by which these sample surveys are conducted. We will report our conclusions as soon as we have had an opportunity to complete our review of this material.

Sincerely,

Lester R. Frankel
Lazare Teper

Frederick F. Stephan
Chairman
Special Advisory Committee
on Employment Statistics

APPENDIX 3

Report of Panel on CENSUS STATISTICS ON THE LABOR FORCE to the INTENSIVE REVIEW COMMITTEE

Introductory Comments

It is scarcely open to controversy that the preparation and release of current, prompt, accurate data on total employment and unemployment in the United States is a necessary responsibility in our present-day industrialized society. Obviously none other than a governmental agency is physically equipped or otherwise in position to perform this task. Furthermore, if the figures are to be accepted as unbiased by all segments of the public, they must be produced by the Government.

The Nation needs comprehensive totals measuring both employment and unemployment, for these are among the broadest indicators of economic change. Such indicators are essential to public and private administration for innumerable purposes. This assumption is generally accepted. Therefore, the task of the panel is to review whether the specific information collected by the Census Bureau meets public and private needs, and how it can be improved, or whether other sources of such data could be substituted.

There are of course, two separate and distinct methods for getting information on the labor force. The two types of data are (1) those secured by household interviews, and (2) those compiled from reports by employers. Each, in its own right, throws light on a different aspect of the labor force, and in turn serves different though complementary uses. In part, these differences arise from the ways in which the basic information can be gathered. In part, they are reflected in the types of use to which data are put.

Labor force information is provided by the Census primarily by means of household surveys. Decennially and historically the Census has conducted periodic across-the-board enumerations of the entire population of the United States (as required by the Constitution) and in doing so has made a comprehensive inventory of the Nation's manpower and its distribution by age, sex, and skill, by occupation and industry, by States and small geographical subdivisions.

The information thus provided by the decennial enumeration is basic, both in its completeness and in the matter of geographic and other detail. Because of its detail and completeness, the taking of a decennial census and the tabulation and publication of its results is a slow, cumbersome, and very costly project, but nevertheless a highly essential one. However, to ascertain promptly the subsequent changes in magnitude and distribution of the employed and unemployed, the decennial censuses must be supplemented by current information on labor force developments, produced on a sample basis. This is being done by the Bureau of the Census as a part of its Current Population Survey.

At the present stage of statistical development in this country, only the Census Bureau's monthly labor force survey is able to provide inclusive national aggregates covering employed and unemployed on a comparable basis -- data for which there is a great need -- and it was for this reason that this project was initiated more than a decade ago. It provides comparable estimates of the unduplicated number of wage and salary employees in industry, Government, and agriculture, and number of self-employed and unpaid family workers in both industry and agriculture, and the number of unemployed persons seeking jobs. At least for the United States as a whole, the country has available an estimate each month of its total civilian labor force including seasonal entrants and withdrawals, and a breakdown into some of its main categories -- particularly employment and unemployment.

For obvious reasons, such data can only be secured on a recurrent monthly basis from a small but adequate sample of households -- not from employer reports.

Since the Monthly Report on the Labor Force is based on a sample of households, it is also a vehicle which enables us to have estimates for a current date of certain characteristics of the labor force which are otherwise only available at the time of decennial censuses. For example, it can tell us the number of housewives who also have outside jobs, the occupational group to which a worker belongs, e.g., skilled craftsmen, clerical workers, etc. (as contrasted with industry grouping, e.g., steel manufacturing, petroleum refining, etc.). That a vehicle for estimates between decennial census years is necessary, particularly to the Government, is also self-apparent. It can also provide us with information on the duration of unemployment, the extent of part-time work, the number of dual job-holders, etc.

In time of mobilization, or when labor supply is tight for other reasons, Government manpower officials and others concerned with labor-market conditions need to know not only the composition of the country's work force, but also such factors as ages, previous occupational status, and marital status of persons currently outside the labor force, e.g., the millions of housewives, students, retired older people, etc. In periods of economic slackness, they want to know who are the unemployed, how long they have been unemployed, and which persons have left the labor market.

The household interviews which supply the raw materials both for the decennial censuses and the current labor force surveys are as essential as the important but different body of data obtained from employing establishments by the U. S. Bureau of Labor Statistics and its cooperating State agencies -- State labor departments, and State employment security agencies which are under the aegis of the U. S. Bureau of Employment Security.

The type of information provided by U.S.B.L.S. portrays monthly changes in the number of employees on the payrolls in the nonagricultural industries. This establishment information is available for individual industries, States, and major labor market areas, and is secured by direct reports from employers. In addition to the number of employees on payrolls, these reports provide information on the number of man-hours paid for as well as the amounts disbursed in payrolls. This in turn permits the computation of data on average weekly earnings, average hourly earnings, and average hours of work. The comprehensive body of data secured in this form thus provides detailed information by industry and locality and is consequently of great importance for pinpointing changes in economic and labor conditions. It is also indispensable for consumer market research purposes.

Household surveys are expensive to the Government on a per unit basis, as compared with employer reporting. This would make prohibitive a household sample large enough to provide reliable monthly estimates of number of employees in a host of detailed industry classifications,* as well as for each State, and for a long list of localities -- as is now done under the U.S.B.L.S. system of employer reports.

---

*It is questionable whether household respondents can provide the kind of detailed industry information which is exemplified by the breakdown adopted by the Federal Government in its Standard Industrial Classification.

The labor market area covered by the establishment data reported by employers to U.S.B.L.S. is tremendous -- about 48 or 49 million employees out of a civilian labor force which this year reached a seasonal peak of nearly 65 million. Nevertheless, there is a large gap, as measured by the difference between these two figures. In part, this informational gap is filled in by other agencies than the Census, but not on a comparable basis statistically. For example, agricultural employment estimates which are prepared by the Department of Agriculture include for its purposes all persons who in a particular reporting week devote any time to agricultural work, even though their major employment in that period may have been nonagricultural.

The only monthly data on the self-employed or unpaid family workers in nonagricultural enterprises are those produced by the Census Bureau.

Although data on unemployment insurance recipients are compiled by the U. S. Department of Labor and the States, they are as yet of limited coverage. Because of this and other technical statistical difficulties, they do not measure the total number of unemployed in the United States seeking work at a particular time.

While the monthly employment, hours, and earnings data produced under the U.S.B.L.S. system of employer reports for the nonagricultural industries are indispensable for their important purposes, they cannot meet the need filled by the household reporting system of the Census Bureau. The U.S.B.L.S. figures contain some duplication, e.g., within a reporting week an employee may appear on the payrolls of two reporting nonagricultural establishments, or he may have worked on a farm as well as in a nonagricultural establishment.

Furthermore, employer reports are based on place of employment rather than residence of employee, and they contain only totals for an establishment without distinction as to age, skill, marital status, etc. To provide such breakdowns would be burdensome and prohibitive to reporting businessmen, and also so time-consuming as to delay reporting. Only the household interview system of the Census Bureau is a feasible one for providing such essential facts, and at the same time securing labor force totals which exclude double-counting of individuals.

From the above, it is obvious that the country needs a complete count of labor force at least every ten years because in this way one is able on a resident basis to find out all the pertinent details of its composition, not only by State, but by county and by city and locality (rural, urban, and suburban). Not only are such data valuable to Government, labor, and industry, but they serve a great consumer market research need.

Since ten years (or even a year) is an impossibly long period for a modern industrial country to remain in the dark as to changes in the broad components of its labor force, the monthly sample and report on the labor force of the Census Bureau fills an obvious need. The decennial census supplies a much too infrequent but absolutely necessary control and check on this sample. For obvious reasons, the decennial census should be as accurate and complete as possible.

The decennial census is the sole source of a comprehensive inventory of the Nation's manpower and its distribution, by age, sex, and skill, by occupation and industry, by States and small areas. It is only from this source that we can determine the rate of labor force participation in the Nation's work. This task has acquired new urgency under the existing conditions of continuing stress and international tension, in estimating manpower resources in relation to military and industrial requirements. The inclusive decennial census and the monthly samples are natural partners in this task of measurement, for the delays and cumbersomeness of the broad and detailed counts are offset by the quick evidence of current changes as provided by the current national sample.

Meanwhile, just as the Census household-visit data supply needed facts on the occupational and work status of the people, so the establishment reports supply the facts on industry and location. Thus, the pieces fit together into the whole. Despite some inevitable discrepancies, each of the parts is essential, and proper attention to technical improvements can produce increasing coordination of end over-all figures as well as detail.

Certain labor force data, e.g., number of proprietors, number of employees, total payroll disbursements, and in the case of manufacturing the man-hours of work, are provided by the Censuses of Manufactures, Trade, Services, and Agriculture, whenever they are taken. Inasmuch as these are complete censuses and not samples, they provide a wealth of localized data on employment, and workers' earnings, which at the same time can be tied up with sales and other measures of production. In manufacturing, by getting all the feasible measures of physical production, in conjunction with the man-hours figures and employment figures, one is able periodically to get a more complete and reliable picture of the productivity of certain industries.

Recommendations

Based on careful deliberations, this panel submits in schematic form below its judgment and recommendations regarding Census statistics relating to the labor force. This judgment, summarized on the basis of thorough group discussion, represents long experience of panel members and their associates in utilizing the statistics of employment and unemployment by business and industry, labor organizations, private research institutions, and Government.

I. Labor Force Information in the Decennial Census

The decennial census is the only source which provides a comprehensive inventory of the Nation's manpower and its essential social and economic characteristics. Thorough coverage of the labor force characteristics of the population should be continued and improved by the Bureau of the Census. The following principles are important in this connection:

A. Since the decennial census is the only comprehensive source of information on small areas and occupational detail, complete enumeration cannot be replaced by the sampling approach. Only a complete enumeration can provide a pinpointed description of the country's manpower, according to locality, major industrial groups, detailed occupations, age, sex, income, etc.

B. Comprehensive decennial figures on the labor force are necessary as "benchmarks" from which to develop current up-to-date figures by means of current household enumerations on a sample basis.

C. The extent to which the population is engaged in the Nation's work is the most important over-all economic and sociological fact needed for periodic appraisal of manpower resources and requirements. This is not only true in ordinary times, but it is particularly so under continuing conditions of stress and international tension where military and industrial manpower needs must be under constant and close examination.

D. Some of the general data are essential background for developing current information on the national aspects of the labor force. However, much of the detailed information is indispensable as a yardstick and benchmark for numerous current regional and local analyses -- many of them conducted outside the Federal agencies by State and local governments, by public and private agencies, as well as by business and labor and agricultural organizations. Thus, the information on the work force must be made available in occupational and geographical detail to serve as an important guide for public and private local action in many fields.

II. Monthly Labor Force Statistics Collected in the Current Population Survey

While the decennial census provides the starting point for analysis of labor force activity and manpower utilization, with a complete and detailed inventory of the Nation's human resources, the current data are necessarily provided only by sampling. In turn, the sample data permit only the development, on a satisfactorily reliable basis, of the more generalized national information on labor force. Certain localized information can be obtained by the use of the household-visit approach, but this involves more adequate hence larger samples for specific localities than are now included in the national household sample. To secure such information regularly for a long list of localities would mean prohibitive expense, so it should be restricted to occasional specific problem situations of such public importance that extra expense is justified. The following principles should be recognized:

A. Monthly data on unemployment, employment, and the labor force are essential tools for current analysis of the economy and for detecting changes in general business and labor conditions. They are also important in the work of the Government in fulfilling its obligations under the Employment Act of 1946.

B. Current data on the labor force obviously should be obtained as an integral part of current population surveys on a sample basis, as is now done under the household survey method used by the Census Bureau. This is inherently the most efficient, fast, and inexpensive way of obtaining an over-all national breakdown of population and labor force into its major subdivisions.

It also makes possible needed analysis in combination with interrelated data on the economic status of the population. The data produced by this method are essential in their own right and cannot be replaced (or replace) the current monthly employee data provided by other governmental agencies through employer reports. (The latter constitute the most efficient, fast, and inexpensive way of producing accurate figures on employee changes in specific, detailed industry classifications and by localities.)

C. Consideration should be given to strengthening the household sample method used by the Census Bureau to obtain general labor force information, so as to assure its reliability. A stronger and otherwise improved sample may be necessary to reflect the growth of suburbanization, industrial decentralization and shifts, etc. This problem should be under continuous scrutiny so that necessary adjustments in sampling will be effectively made with the least possible delay in order to maintain a truly representative national character.

D. Additional detail when needed should be added to the standard items included in the regular survey. For example, there are periods when it is to the national interest to know what workers are leaving or entering the labor force, and why they are doing so. There are times when we need to have special information on population currently outside the labor force -- their previous work experience, skills, age, sex, marital status, etc.

III. Biennial Census of Manufactures a needed source of Labor Data

The periodic business censuses on an establishment basis are of outstanding importance to business, labor, and the public generally. Of greatest importance is the need for frequent and complete information on the highly sensitive sector represented by manufacturing in order to reflect changing conditions in this most dynamic and volatile part of the economy. Employment and man-hour information is important here because it links directly with reports on output for the same establishments (essential for measurement of productivity), with reports on wages paid and value added by manufactures. The relatively high degree of interindustry uniformity in Census of Manufactures data adds to its usefulness in analysis of the economy as compared with information designed more immediately for individual industry use. Such data are also invaluable for the preparation of national income data and related national accounts.

The Census program for the current collection of information from business establishments should give priority to a resumption of the biennial Census of Manufactures, as was done between 1919 and 1939. Such biennial censuses will provide employment and related data on a uniform and comprehensive basis in conjunction with production data.

Without a biennial Census of Manufactures, it becomes necessary for statisticians to extrapolate basic series from sample data which are too remote from benchmarks -- a dangerous practice. The annual Survey of Manufactures, which is conducted on a sample basis, does not satisfy the needs for labor market analysis and evaluation, particularly on a localized basis. Furthermore, the results have thus far seemed subject to many sampling errors on an individual industry basis.

IV. Income Statistics

Data on annual personal incomes offer an important measure of economic status. Besides, incomes are the main product of labor force activity. These statistics should therefore continue to be gathered at the decennial censuses as well as annually on a sample basis through the Current Population Survey and its Monthly Report on the Labor Force.

There are, of course, technical difficulties when certain types of income other than wages and salaries are involved. There are problems regarding the accuracy of information on all types of incomes, since it is affected by the ability of the respondents in household enumerations to recollect or know the exact facts about total money income earned by each member of the family over an entire year. Nor do the Census figures cover non-monetary incomes. Serious questions may be raised, therefore, regarding the reliability of the resulting income figures. That is why additional techniques must be devised to reduce the degree of error in these inquiries in order to prevent any possible bias in the figures. Furthermore, the deficiencies of the data, to the extent that they are known and even if all of them cannot be measured precisely, should be clearly explained in the presentation of the information. There is also a need to clarify the relationship of this information to other national accounts.

V. Technical Improvements

The panel commends the high degree of competence of the Census personnel and the degree of achievement it attains in processing and analysis of data. The present efforts to improve the basic data and to extend comparability with related sources should be intensified. The panel offers the following suggestions:

A. As the fact-finding agency, the Census should recognize that the work status of the labor force is not adequately described by simplified subdivision between the employed and the unemployed. For example, there is a question whether a person laid off for thirty days or less but expecting to return to his former job and not looking for other employment, should be classified as "employed" as is the current practice, or as "unemployed." To identify this middle group more clearly would constitute not so much a recognition of its controversial character, as a recognition of the need for dealing with such categories in different ways for different purposes at different times. The Census Bureau's analyses and reports should provide sufficient information in this and other twilight zones to facilitate classification within the labor force to meet various purposes and to prevent misunderstanding by the general public.

B. Technical work on definitions and concepts should be continued. In particular, consideration should be given to development of more detailed information on the twilight zones between employment and unemployment, and equally important is further work in reducing the zone of uncertainty that exists between "labor force" and those "outside of it" in present statistical measurement.

C. Additional efforts should be made to insure the representativeness of the monthly census figures on the labor force and to safeguard their adequacy and sensitivity for the portrayal of the month-to-month changes in over-all national employment and unemployment. This requires the fullest cooperation with other collecting and analytical agencies -- particulary with the U. S. Bureau of Labor Statistics, and also with the U. S. Department of Agriculture. Such coordinated review is all the more important because the information produced by the different agencies throws light on different aspects of employment, unemployment, and the general work status of our population. The public interest in the adequacy of data is always important, but particularly so during periods of economic uncertainty. Every effort is therefore called for, and a continued, reasonable expenditure of public funds is justified to assure measures sufficiently sensitive to economic change. The Census Bureau must continue the re-examination of definitions of the employed and unemployed, to insure optimum utility of data for labor market analysis, and to make its figures properly sensitive to meaningful changes in current economic conditions.

D. The monthly sample should of course be sufficiently adequate to provide at all times the basic general national breakdowns nowadays presented by the Census Bureau in its current monthly reports on the labor force. However, at best, the regular monthly sample cannot be large enough to provide reliably many more detailed cross-tabulations between various demographic factors (age, sex, marital status, etc.) and the individual's status within or outside the labor force. Yet there is a national need for such cross-tabulations on special occasions. At such times, consideration should be given to a temporary expansion of the sample to a size which would reliably provide these cross-tabulations. This is essential for the accuracy of detailed analyses into the composition and changing structure of the Nation's labor force.

E. Adaptation of definitions and tabulations to analytical uses requires further refinement. This can best be brought about by continued consultation with users of data. An important example of needed refinement is found in the case of the information presented on average weekly hours of work. If such data are to be presented, they should distinguish the hours of wage and salaried employees from those of the self-employed and unpaid family workers.

F. The broad groupings of occupations in the decennial censuses and in the monthly report on the labor force appear to be too general for many uses. Some subdivisions in the interest of greater homogeneity and clarity are definitely indicated. Insofar as individual occupations are concerned, there is a continued need to make sure that job-titles do not become obsolescent due to changing technology and industrial patterns.

Conclusion

We believe that the uses of labor force statistics are as manifold and extensive as the uses of population data. In our opinion, it would be impossible to allocate costs of production of these basic data to specific users, public or private. The publication of the data should be broad and complete as a direct charge against Federal tax revenues. (This is not intended to preclude the regular charges of the Government Printing Office.) Only in the case of special requests for tabulations which are not of general interest can costs be properly assessed by the Census Bureau against an agency or an individual requesting such special service. Once the Census Bureau has been reimbursed for providing such a special tabulation, ~~the material should then~~ be available to the general public on request.

When budgetary stringencies arise, recurrent sample collections are likely to be suggested as the first casualty in the search for economies. This is natural because a complete decennial census is the basic inventory and therefore the rockbottom requirement. It is to be hoped that such a hazard does not exist in the case of the monthly sample on labor force, and its component elements of employment and unemployment. Such an event would be very unfortunate, and would deprive the Nation and the Government of an important source of vital information.

The Census Bureau is the agency charged with the complete decennial count of labor force as well as of total population. It is also the government agency which has had the most experience in the household enumeration technique. We believe, therefore, that, under the existing conditions, the present division of responsibility between the Census Bureau and the Bureau of Labor Statistics in the production of statistical data should not be altered. There exists, of course, a crying need for a better integration of labor force data released by the two agencies, each of which has special competence in its own sphere.

The need for such coordination is all the more essential inasmuch as occasional apparent contradictions appear between the two sets of data as a result of conceptual or other differences. The Census Bureau and the Bureau of Labor Statistics (and also the Bureau of Agricultural Economics) must cooperate more closely than heretofore in this field so as to eliminate every possible source of public confusion. Each agency should moreover cooperate by giving a continuous and close scrutiny to its respective operations in order to ascertain what further improvements are needed to produce reasonably harmonious data on the labor force and its activity.

PANEL ON CENSUS STATISTICS ON THE LABOR FORCE

Cedric Wolfe, Chairman
Metropolitan Life Insurance Company
Solomon Barkin
Textile Workers Union of America
Martin Gainsbrugh
National Industrial Conference Board
Meredith B. Givens
Division of Placement & Unemployment Insurance of New York State
Peter Henle
American Federation of Labor
Howard B. Myers
Committee for Economic Development

November 14, 1953

APPENDIX 4

Bureau of the Census Statement on Decision to Change to 230-area Design for Current Population Survey

Although work had been in progress for more than two years on the sampling aspects of the 230-area design for CPS, most of the discussions concerning the timing and method of transition and its feasibility in terms of budgetary and other considerations started in the fall of 1952 and the early part of 1953. The prospect of a Census of Business in 1954 led to a decision to expand the retail trade survey to the 230 areas, for operations during 1953 would provide a measure of the effect on total sales of establishments going out of business during the Census year and a measure of the quality of the Census itself. In addition, it was anticipated that once operations in the 230 areas had been established it would be feasible to give up the 68-area design for the retail trade survey and continue to collect the current monthly reports from the new sample.

There was little disagreement about the desirability and even the necessity of an expansion in sample coverage for the CPS under favorable circumstances. Unfortunately, because the measures of sampling variability for the old sample were inadequate, the gains in reliability from the new design were understated initially. Along with budgetary problems, the apparently small gains involved for many important items had led to some delays on reaching agreement for making the transition.

A good deal of staff time during the winter and early spring of 1953 was devoted to a study of operating procedures and budget estimates for the new design. It was recognized that the proposed wider spread of the sample would lead to increased travel costs, and an effort was made to find ways, through changes in operating methods, to carry the improvements in the design of both CPS and the retail trade survey at approximately the same total cost of operation as in the 68-area sample. This study led to the conclusion that more effective use could be made of the supervisory organization by operating out of 34 District Offices rather than the 63 in the 68-area design. With this organization, the number of District Supervisors and Assistants could correspondingly be reduced from 81 to 63, with a similar reduction in supporting full-time District Office personnel and with the number of Regional Offices reduced from 7 to 5. It was proposed that in carrying through these changes steps would be taken to adapt and introduce in field operations recent methods for statistical quality control.

These changes would lead to somewhat fewer supervisors who would have to travel more widely to carry out their functions, but with stronger and better paid supervisory positions on the average. They also meant that supervisors who formerly spent a portion of their time doing actual interviewing and office work would be devoting their energies more fully to the supervisory aspects of the job. (In the 68-area design, the CPS enumeration in almost half the District Offices typically required less than 4 enumerators.) With these changes it was expected that total operating costs under the new design would remain about the same as for the 68-area sample.

While the 230-area design was expected to operate under about the same budget as the old, once a transition was made, any approach to carrying through the transition was costly and would require additional funds. The planning for the transition was considered as a separate problem, and its own budget established. Allowance was made for funds which could have been properly allocated for this purpose from the appropriations originally anticipated. The original plans for the transition were made on the assumption that most of the existing offices would continue during the period of introducing the new sample.

The initial action of the House of Representatives in May 1953 in denying funds for the Economic Censuses, and for planning for the Census of Agriculture, required both a reappraisal of the current program operations at that time and of the redesign. Staff reductions were necessary. It was decided to reduce immediately the field organization to the levels indicated above, to reduce the retail trade survey in the 230 areas from the level of an 8 percent sample to 6 percent, and to eliminate operation of the retail trade survey in the 68 areas. A staggered reduction down to 34 field offices was begun in June and completed by August 30. The final decision of the Congress in the summer of 1953 to provide funds for spot checks again changed the situation, and a transition of the CPS to the new design appeared once more to be possible.

The proposed method of making the transition also went through a period of evolution during the spring and summer of the year. Somewhat earlier, consideration had been given to a large-scale pretest of the new type of field organization (involving several offices each of which would handle several scattered p.s.u.'s) in order to develop and test various operating procedures, to develop more adequate cost estimates, and even possibly to institute checking devices for rough comparisons of quality between the old and the new systems. Because of budgetary and time considerations, this proposal was put aside in favor of a limited dry-run of the new organization in one new office (Houston) starting in September.

There was also some original sentiment for introducing the new design gradually, perhaps 10 percent a month, over a period of a year to a year and a half. Each new 10 percent part, under this proposal, would have been on a dry-run basis for a month or two and would then have replaced a comparable part of the old design. This proposal was finally dropped because it made it difficult to determine for a substantial period of time (and one in which significant economic developments were predicted by many) whether month-to-month changes represented actual trends or merely the impact of the transition.

The final decision, then, was to accomplish the transition over a relatively short period of time, but one adequate for training purposes and for some overlap measurements of differences between the two designs. A description of the actual method of transition is already available to the committee.

It was recognized that the proposed method of transition entailed certain risks. These resulted from the necessity for carrying through the transition with limited funds, and from the fact that the reduced field staff would have the responsibility for continuing the 68-area survey in full and simultaneously undertaking the extensive work on recruitment, training, and sample selection for the new design. All of these activities were compressed into a few months. Inherent in the decision was the assumption that the experienced enumerators on the old operation would continue to turn in satisfactory work with a minimum of supervisory attention and with mail training only. A program of mail training was developed for this purpose. It was also planned to supplement the field staff during the transition period with Washington personnel qualified to assume some of the burden of training of new enumerators.

In spite of actual developments, these assumptions in retrospect still do not appear unreasonable. There was some apprehension about cutting out offices prior to accomplishing the transition and some feeling that not enough emphasis was being given to maintenance of the old operation. However, the degree of deterioration in the results from the old sample came as almost a complete surprise. The same could be said for the apparent success in achieving so satisfactory a level of enumeration in the new sample in so short a period of time. If anything, it was conjectural whether the new staff in the 230 sample areas would provide adequate measurements by the end of the transition period, regardless of what happened in the old operation.

A chronology of events associated with the transition is given below:

1. February 1953, Institution of expanded retail trade program. The retail trade survey was extended into 230 p.s.u.'s in February 1953, still retaining the 68-area

trade survey as well. Although the supervisory staff was required to recruit and train a new staff of enumerators for this purpose and undertake many other associated functions, the timing of the work was such as not to conflict with the regular CPS enumeration period each month. Enumerator turnover in the new areas was much higher than had been anticipated with the result that recruiting and retraining costs in this new operation were larger than expected for the early months. A reappraisal of the Bureau's overall budgetary position resulted in some curtailment even in CPS training in the last month or two of the fiscal year.

2. May 1953, Elimination of Economic Censuses. In May, the House of Representatives passed the Census appropriation bill without making provision for the scheduled Censuses of Business and Manufactures or for planning funds for the Census of Agriculture. With some cuts impending even in funds for current surveys, it was decided to make a reduction in the number of field offices and a sharp reduction-in-force in Washington, in order to preserve whatever funds were appropriated for fiscal 1954 from being depleted more than necessary by accumulated annual leave and duty notices to employees being terminated.

3. July 1953, Spot-check program. In July, the Congress formally completed action on the appropriations, providing, in addition to current survey funds, $1,500,000 for spot checks in lieu of the Economic Censuses. The retention of the 230-area operation for the retail trade survey was assured and the final plan for the CPS transition, described earlier in this memorandum was drawn up. The plans required the use of spot-check funds and also assumed the savings resulting from the reduction in field offices.

4. August 1953, Reduction in field offices and end of direct training in old design. The reduction to 34 field offices was instituted in June and completed by August 30. With some strengthening of the remaining offices, the relative reduction in the number of District and Assistant District Supervisors was proportionately smaller than the reduction in offices as shown in the attached table which compares field organization on May 1, 1953 and May 1, 1954. There was, however, a limited amount of additional displacement of experienced supervisors by inexperienced personnel because many did not have Civil Service status and a few of these

were dislodged from their positions by displaced career workers from other agencies. A few others would not accept new positions in the new locations because of the danger of displacement. Some gain was realized in certain specific instances where staff of marginal ability were not retained in the new organization. August was also the last month in which any formal group training sessions were held for enumerators in the old design. In about 15 old p.s.u.'s which no longer had offices, one enumerator was designated as a "senior enumerator" and given additional duties. The duties were confined primarily to inquiries (probably by telephone) on whether other enumerators had received their assignments and mail training materials, understood the materials, and were prepared to carry out their assignments.

5. <u>September-October 1953, Dry-run started in Houston and Field conferences on redesign.</u> In September, a dry-run was instituted in the Houston office (with 6 new p.s.u.'s) to continue until the end of the year, primarily to develop and test field operating and training procedures. Washington personnel participated in the dry-run and a number of changes and improvements arose as a result of this experience. Most other offices were also engaged in geographic and listing work associated with selection of the new sample in other p.s.u.'s. Conferences of District Supervisors attended also by Washington personnel were held in each Region in the last week of September. The detailed plan and time schedule for achieving the CPS transition was discussed at length and Supervisors were instructed to recruit enumerators (enlisting the retail trade enumerators where feasible) and set up the prescribed training sessions for those to be used in the November dry-run in one-third of the new p.s.u.'s. Listing and other geographic work continued in the field.

6. <u>November 1953-January 1954, Institution of redesign on dry-run basis.</u> A description of this phase of the transition is already available to the committee. Some Washington personnel were assigned temporarily to the field to assist in the training operation, and attention was directed almost exclusively to the needs of the new operation. The situation was intensified by considerably greater problems than had been anticipated in recruitment and retention of the new enumerators. However, in spite of the knowledge of many that the old operation would shortly be discontinued, there was little turnover in the old enumerator staff during this period.

Comparison of Field Organization

63 Offices - May 1, 1953
34 Offices - May 1, 1954

Personnel	May 1, 1953			May 1, 1954		
	Auth.	Actual	Vacancies	Auth.	Actual	Vacancies
Regional Supervisors.........	7	7	0	5	5	0
Asst. Regional Supervisors...	7	6	1	5	3*	2
Regional Secretaries.........	7	7	0	5	5	0
Regional Field Assistants....	3	3	0	3	3	0
Regional Total............	24	23	1	18	16	2
District Supervisors.........	63	59	4	34	33	1
Asst. District Supervisors...	19	17	2	26	23	3
District Office Sub-total.	82	76	6	60	56	4
Program Supervisors (GS-7,8).	1	1	0	2	2	0
Supervisory Clerks (GS-4,5)..	6	5	1	34	32	2
Clerk-Typists (GS-3).........	69	65	4	39	37	2
Cotton Office Personnel...... (½ time)	6	6	0	2	2	0
District Office Total.....	164	153	11	137	129	8
Grand Total...........	188	176	12	155	145	10

The above does not include field staff employed solely on Trust Fund work.

* Includes 1 acting

Bureau of the Census
May 28, 1954

A P P E N D I X 5

CONCEPTS AND METHODS USED IN THE CURRENT LABOR FORCE STATISTICS PREPARED BY THE BUREAU OF THE CENSUS[1]

(This report supersedes Current Population Reports, Labor Force, "Labor Force Memorandum No. 5," issued November 8, 1950. It incorporates changes in methods and procedures instituted in the Current Population Survey since that date, primarily in sample design and estimation procedure)

Current information on employment, unemployment, and related data are compiled each month from the Current Population Survey of the Bureau of the Census. This survey is conducted each month with a scientifically selected sample representing the noninstitutional civilian population. The results are announced in the Combined Employment and Unemployment Release issued jointly by the Departments of Commerce and Labor; the joint release, issued as a press statement, presents the information from the survey together with related data from the Department of Labor. Fuller details from the Current Population Survey are issued in the Bureau of the Census "The Monthly Report on the Labor Force," Current Population Reports, Series P-57. A discussion of the underlying concepts and a description of the methods used in the preparation of these statistics follow.

CONCEPTS

The concepts of the labor force and unemployment used in the Bureau of the Census Current Population Survey were introduced in the latter stages of the depression of the thirties, chiefly in the interest of deriving more objective measurements of unemployment and employment than were previously available.

Prior to the thirties, aside from attempts in some of the decennial censuses, there were no direct measurements of the number of jobless persons. With the development of mass unemployment in the early thirties, widely conflicting estimates began to make their appearance. As a consequence, many research groups, as well as State and municipal governments, began experimenting with direct surveys of the population or samples of the population. In these surveys, an attempt was made to classify the population as in or out of the labor force or as employed or unemployed by means of various series of questions addressed to each individual. In most of the surveys, the unemployed were defined as those who were not working but were "willing and able" to work. This concept, however, did not meet the standards of objectivity that many technicians felt were necessary in order to measure not only the level of unemployment at one time but changes over periods of time. The criterion "willing and able to work," when applied in specific situations, appeared too intangible and too dependent upon the interpretation and attitude of the person being interviewed.

Out of this experimentation, there was developed in the late thirties a set of concepts which sought to meet these various criticisms. According to these concepts, the classification of an individual was to be dependent principally upon his actual activity, i.e., whether working or looking for work, or doing something else, within a designated time

[1] This appendix is a reprint of the Bureau of the Census, Current Population Report, Series P-23, No. 2, issued July 30, 1954.

period. Although there have been improvements in measurement techniques, these concepts have been used, in substantially unchanged form, in the 1940 Census, in the Current Population Survey, and in the 1950 Census.

In measuring activity, the time period selected for the monthly survey was a calendar week. Several considerations led to adopting a calendar week as the time reference for the surveys. First of all, the period used must be short enough so that the data obtained would be "current" and so that the time reference would not tax the memory of the person giving the information. Second, it must not be so short that the occurrence of holidays or other accidental events would cause extremely erratic fluctuations in the information obtained. A calendar week seemed to fulfill these conditions as well as being a convenient and easily defined period of time.

The criteria used in classifying persons on the basis of their activity are described below:

Labor force.--The labor force comprises all civilians who are employed or unemployed, and persons in the Armed Forces. Since the number of persons in the Armed Forces is available from official records, the monthly survey is confined to the civilian population. The data relate to persons 14 years old and over. In the United States most children under 14 do relatively little work because of laws which restrict child labor, laws regarding compulsory school attendance, and general social custom.

Employed persons.--Employed persons comprise (1) all those who, during the specified week, did any work at all as paid employees or in their own business or profession, or on their own farm, or who worked 15 hours or more as unpaid workers on a farm or in a business operated by a member of the family, and (2) all those who were not working or looking for work but who had jobs or businesses from which they were temporarily absent because of illness, bad weather, vacation, labor-management dispute, or because they were temporarily laid off with definite instructions to return to work within 30 days of layoff. Also included are persons who had acquired new jobs or were about to begin new enterprises, at which they were scheduled to start work within 30 days. Excluded from the employed group are persons whose only activity consisted of work around the house (such as own home housework, painting or repairing own home, etc.) or volunteer work for religious, charitable, and similar organizations.

Unemployed.--This group includes all persons who did no work at all (as defined above) in the survey week and who were looking for work. Those who had made efforts to find jobs within the preceding 60-day period--such as by registering at a public or private employment agency, writing letters of application, canvassing for work, etc.--and who, during the survey week, were awaiting the results of these efforts are also regarded as looking for work. Included with the unemployed, although they were not actually looking for work, are certain special groups known as the "inactive unemployed." These are persons who report they would have been looking for work except that they were temporarily ill, they were awaiting recall to a job from which they were on indefinite layoff or layoff exceeding 30 days, or they believed no work was available in their line of work or in the community. These groups are included since, under particular circumstances, such persons, although genuinely in the market for jobs, are not likely to be actively looking for work.

DATA PUBLISHED

Every month, estimates of the employment status of the population 14 years old and over are published in "The Monthly Report on the Labor Force," Current Population Reports, Series P-57. Estimates of the labor force, agricultural and nonagricultural employment, unemployment, and persons outside the labor force are shown by age and sex. For the employed, estimates of those actually at work at their jobs during the survey week and those with jobs but not at work are published separately. A distribution of hours worked during the survey week is given for those at work. Those with jobs but not at work are classified according to the reason for not working. Duration of unemployment is shown for those seeking work. The regular monthly report is usually issued about three weeks after collection of the data and is either preceded by or issued simultaneously with the Combined Employment and Unemployment Release mentioned earlier.

The regular labor force survey is supplemented by a program of additional inquiries, coordinated with the monthly enumerations, which is designed to provide more detailed statistics on special problems in order to help qualify and interpret the broad over-all totals published each month. The results of these studies are usually published in Current Population Reports, Series P-50. For example, because of the usefulness of such data in diagnosing economic trends, information is now being obtained each quarter on the characteristics of part-time workers. From these studies, estimates are published on the number and characteristics of those working part time because of slack work, job turnover, unavailability of full-time jobs and other economic factors, as well as those working part time from choice or for various personal reasons. Another important item made available from these quarterly studies is the number of unemployed persons looking for part-time rather than full-time work.

Other supplementary inquiries are used to measure the number of workers holding more than one job and in more than one industry; annual income of persons and families; the size of the group working at any time during the period of a year; the earnings and labor input of farm wage workers during the year; and similar economic phenomena. Through these supplementary inquiries, as well as the detail provided in the monthly statistics, it is possible to regroup various categories of persons in different ways to provide, for example, measures of unemployment or employment under alternative definitions.

THE SURVEY DESIGN

The Current Population Survey sample is spread over 230 sample areas comprising 453 counties and independent cities. A total of 24,000 to 26,000 dwelling units and other living quarters are designated for the sample at any time, and completed interviews are obtained each month from about 20,000 to 22,000 households. Of the remainder, about 500 to 1,000 are households from which information should be collected but is not because the occupants are not found at home after repeated calls, are temporarily absent, or are unavailable for other reasons. The other 2,500 to 3,500 designated units represent those found to be vacant, occupied by persons with residences elsewhere, or otherwise not to be enumerated. The over-all sample size varies over time, partly because of chance but also because of the growth of the population and the creation of new households. Every two to three years, as the sample expands with population growth, it is necessary to decrease the sampling ratio slightly in order to keep the workload at the average of roughly 25,000 designated units prescribed under the survey budget.

Selection of sample areas.--The entire area of the United States consisting of about 3,000 counties was divided into about 2,000 primary sampling units. With some minor exceptions, a primary sampling unit (PSU) consists of a county or a number of contiguous counties. Each standard metropolitan area (SMA) constituted a separate PSU. In combining counties to form PSU's each PSU was defined so as to be as heterogeneous as possible. Greater heterogeneity could be accomplished by including more counties. However, another important consideration was to have the PSU sufficiently compact in area so that a small sample spread throughout it could be efficiently canvassed without undue travel cost. A typical primary unit, for example, included both urban and rural residents of both high and low economic levels and provided, to the extent feasible, diverse occupations and industries.

The PSU's were then grouped into 230 strata. The 44 largest standard metropolitan areas and certain other SMA's were strata by themselves. In general, however, a stratum consisted of a set of PSU's as much alike as possible in various characteristics such as geographic region, population density, rate of growth in the 1940-1950 decade, percentage nonwhite, principal industry, type of agriculture, and so on. These are the same types of criteria used in the stratification of the old 68-area design instituted in 1943 but recently discontinued, although of course more recent information was used. Except for the 44 largest SMA's and the 16 other areas, each of which is a complete stratum, the strata were established so that their sizes in terms of 1950 population were approximately equal. Where a PSU was a stratum by itself, it automatically fell in the sample. From each of the other strata, one PSU was selected in a random manner for inclusion in the sample, the selection having been made in such a manner that the probability of the selection of any one unit was proportionate to its 1950 population. For example, within a stratum the chance that a PSU with a population of 50,000 would be selected was twice that for a unit with a population of 25,000.

The resulting 230 areas are those in which the survey is being conducted.

Selection of sample households.--For each stratum an over-all sampling ratio of about 1 in 2,250 is used at the present time (1954). The sampling ratio used in each particular sample area (sample PSU) depends on the proportion that the sample area population (at the time of the 1950 Census) was of the stratum population. Thus, in a sample area which was one-tenth of the stratum, the within-PSU sampling ratio which results is 1 in 225, achieving the desired ratio of 1 in 2,250 for the stratum.

Within each of the 230 PSU's, area sampling methods are used in the selection of specific households. In each PSU, the number of households to be enumerated each month is determined by the application of the within-PSU sampling ratio rather than through the assignment of a fixed quota. This procedure makes it possible for the sample to reflect any shifts in population. For example, if on the basis of the 1950 Census a sample ratio of 1 in every 225 is used in a sample area, the number of households expected in the sample will be larger than that obtained by a fixed quota in areas where the number of households has increased since the census. In areas where the number of households has declined, the expected number of sample households will be smaller. In this way the sample properly reflects the changing distribution of the population and avoids the distortion which would result from the application of fixed quotas of households, or persons, based on the population at an earlier date.

In the application of area sampling methods, several stages of sampling were used within each selected PSU. First, a sample of administrative units used for the 1950 Censuses of Population and Housing (enumeration districts) was selected, with the probability of selection of any one of these proportionate to its 1950 population. These selected enumeration districts were then subdivided into segments, that is, small land areas with well-defined boundaries having in general an expected "size" of about six dwelling units or other living quarters. Where roads, streams, and other terrain features that could be used to subdivide an enumeration district were insufficient, some of the resultant segments were several times the desired average "size" of six households. For each subdivided enumeration district, one segment was designated for the sample, with the probability of selection proportionate to the estimated "size" of the segment. Where available advance information indicated that the segment contained about six households, all units within the segment boundaries were to be included in the sample. In cases where the advance information indicated a segment "size" of several times six units, a field listing was to be made of all living quarters in the segment and a systematic subsample drawn so as to achieve the equivalent of a segment which is canvassed completely.

In subdividing enumeration districts into segments and in determining in advance the approximate "size" of each segment, use was made of various materials. In the larger urban places, information concerning the number of units in each block was obtained from Block Statistics bulletins published from results of the 1950 Censuses of Population and Housing for 209 of the cities of 50,000 inhabitants or more. In conjunction with these bulletins, considerable use was made of large-scale Sanborn maps, which are available commercially and relatively up-to-date for most medium-size and large urban centers and show the general outline of each structure within blocks. Where such data were not available, the location and number of dwelling units in small geographic areas bounded by roads, streams, etc., were obtained either from maps used by interviewers in the 1950 Censuses of Population and Housing or from special field visits. Enumeration districts in urban centers--where mapping materials were generally more precise--were more readily subdivided into compact segments (averaging six units) than were those in rural areas; but a substantial proportion of the resultant rural segments were of this size also. Some variation in actual segment size arose also where the mapping materials, although sufficiently detailed, were out-of-date because of substantial new construction or because they contained errors.

Rotation of sample.--Part of the sample is changed each month. A primary reason for rotating the sample is to avoid the problems of lack of cooperation which arise when a constant panel is interviewed indefinitely. To accomplish this rotation of the sample on a gradual basis, mapping and other materials for several samples are prepared simultaneously. For each sample, eight systematic subsamples (rotation groups) of segments are identified.

A given rotation group is interviewed for a total of eight months, divided into two equal periods. It is in the sample for four consecutive months one year, leaves the sample during the following eight months, and then returns for the same four calendar months of the next year. In any one month, one-eighth of the sample segments are in their first month of enumeration, another eighth are in their second month, and so on, with the last eighth in for the eighth time (the fourth month of the second period of enumeration). Under this system 75 percent of the sample segments are common from month to month and 50 percent from year to year. This procedure provides a substantial amount of month-to-month and year-to-year overlap in the panel (thus reducing discontinuities in the series of data) without burdening any specific group of households with an unduly long period of inquiry.

Survey techniques.--The immediate field supervisory staff consists of roughly 60 District and Assistant District Supervisors located in 34 centers. During the CPS enumeration period each month, they devote most of their time to control and supervision of the survey, although they have various other assignments during the remainder of the month. They supervise, in total, a staff of about 350 part-time interviewers.

Each month, during the calendar week containing the 15th day, these interviewers contact some responsible person in the sample households in the Current Population Survey. At the time of first enumeration of a household, the interviewer prepares a roster of the household members, including their personal characteristics (date of birth, sex, race, marital status, and veteran status) and their relationship to the household head. This roster is brought up-to-date at each subsequent interview to take account of new or departed residents, changes in marital status, and similar items. The information on personal characteristics is then available each month for identification purposes and for cross-classification with the economic characteristics of the sample population.

At each monthly visit, the interviewer asks a series of standard questions on economic activity during the preceding week (the calendar week containing the eighth day of the month, called the "survey week") for each household member 14 years of age and over. The primary purpose of these questions is to classify the sample population into three basic economic groups--the employed, the unemployed, and those not in the labor force.

Additional questions are asked each month to supplement the basic data. For the employed, information is obtained on hours worked during the survey week, together with a description of the current job, and, for those temporarily away from their jobs, the reason for not working during the survey week. For the unemployed, information is obtained on the length of time they have been looking for work and a description of their last job. For those outside the labor force, their principal activity during the survey week--whether keeping house, going to school, or doing something else--is recorded.

The questionnaires used in the survey are of a special form known as "document-sensing" schedules. Instead of writing down the information, the interviewer, for most items, draws a mark through an oval representing the correct answer, using a special type of pencil. Forms prepared in this fashion can be converted into punchcards by a special document-sensing machine, thus avoiding manual punchcard preparation. The procedure also reduces coding of answers to a minimum, since the position of each oval on the form itself represents a code signal.

ESTIMATION PROCEDURE

The document-sensing schedules (questionnaire forms) containing the information obtained for each person in the sample are received in the Washington office by the week after enumeration. The raw data are converted to punchcards by means of a mechanical document reproducer. Estimates could be prepared by tabulating these cards with a fixed weight (the reciprocal of the sample ratio--approximately 2,250 at present) after accounting for households that were not interviewed. However, to increase the reliability of the labor force statistics derived from the sample, two stages of ratio estimates and a "composite estimate" are used. It is possible to achieve this rather complicated procedure rapidly and automatically because of the availability of the UNIVAC, a high-speed electronic digital computer. The principal steps involved are as given below:

Adjustment for households not interviewed.--The weights for all interviewed households are adjusted to the extent needed to account for occupied households for which no interview was obtained because of absence, impassable roads, refusals, or unavailability for other reasons. This adjustment is made separately for certain groups of PSU's and, within these, for each color (white, nonwhite)-residence (urban, rural nonfarm, rural farm) group of households. The proportion of sample households not interviewed is usually about 3 to 5 percent.

Ratio estimates.--The distribution of the population selected for the sample may differ somewhat from that of the Nation as a whole in such basis characteristics as age, color, sex, and farm-nonfarm residence, among other things. These particular population characteristics are closely correlated with labor force participation and other principal measurements made from the sample. Therefore, some of the sample estimates can be improved substantially when, by appropriate weighting of the original returns, the sample population is brought as closely into agreement as possible with the known distribution of the entire population with respect to these characteristics. Such weighting is accomplished through two stages of ratio estimates as follows:

1. First stage.--The first stage of ratio estimates takes into account differences at the time of the last census in the distribution by color and residence of the population estimated from the sample PSU's and that of the total population in each of the four major regions of the country. Independent distributions of the total population by residence cross-classified by color are not available on a current basis. Instead, using 1950 census data, ratios were developed of the estimated total population by color and residence in a given region based on sample PSU's to the corresponding total population of the region. Such a ratio estimate does not imply that the ratio existing in 1950 would be unchanged at a current date. The estimates from sample PSU's were based on the total census counts, not on sample survey counts. In deriving these ratios, self-representing PSU's were excluded from the computations, since they represent only themselves in the CPS sample. In tabulations of the monthly results from the Current Population Survey, the weights for all sample households from nonselfrepresenting PSU's in a given region are multiplied by the population ratio for that region for the appropriate color-residence class.

2. Second stage.--The second stage of ratio estimates takes account of current differences between the population distributions of the sample and that of the Nation as a whole by age, color, and sex. Independent estimates of the entire population, by these characteristics, are prepared each month. They are calculated by carrying forward the most recent census data (1950) to take account of subsequent aging of the population, mortality, and migration between the United States and other countries.[1] The CPS sample returns (taking into account the weights determined after the first stage of ratio estimates) are, in effect, used to determine only the percentage distribution within a given age-color-sex group by employment status and various other characteristics. In developing statistics in absolute numbers, these percentage distributions are multiplied by the independent population estimate for the appropriate age-color-sex group.

Composite estimate.--The last stage in the preparation of estimates makes use of a composite estimate. In this procedure, a weighted average is obtained of two estimates for the current month for any particular item. The first estimate is the result of the two stages of ratio estimates noted above. The second estimate consists of the composite estimate for the preceding month to which has been added an estimate of the change in each item from the preceding month to the present month based upon that part of the sample which is common to the two months (75 percent). While the weights for the two components of such a composite estimate are not necessarily equal, in this instance the weights used for combining these two estimates are each one-half. Equal weights in this case satisfy the condition that for virtually all items there will be some gain in reliability over the estimation procedure after the first two stages of ratio estimates.

This composite estimate results in a reduction in the sampling error for most important statistics from the survey beyond that achieved after the two stages of ratio estimates described above, and for some items the reduction is substantial. The resultant gains in reliability are greatest in estimates of

[1] See U. S. Bureau of the Census, Current Population Reports, Series P-25, No. 93, April 26, 1954, for a description of the methods used in preparing these independent population estimates.

month-to-month change, although gains are also obtained for estimates of level in a given month or change from year to year or over other intervals of time.

ADEQUACY OF THE DATA

Problems of concept.--As discussed earlier, the basis of the labor force classification used in the Current Population Survey is the activity of an individual during a particular calendar week each month. Obviously, a person could have engaged in more than one activity during the period. Thus, in classifying persons, it is necessary to assign a priority to the various activities for which information was obtained. In this way, an individual is classified in only one group and unduplicated totals of the employed, the unemployed, and persons outside the labor force can be obtained.

In this classification system, the highest priority is assigned to the activity "working." Thus, if a person did any work in the survey week (that is, any work besides home housework or other work around the house or volunteer work) he is classified as "at work" and is included with the employed, even though he may also have looked for work, gone to school, or done something else.

The activity "looking for work" is given second priority in the classification scheme. Thus, if a person did not work at all during the survey week but was looking for work, he is regarded as in the market for a job and is classified as unemployed. In defining the unemployed, a slight departure was made from a strict "activity" concept. It was recognized that, under certain circumstances, some persons, although unemployed in any realistic sense, might not be looking for work continuously. For example, in a 1-plant town, if the plant is shut down most workers would have no alternative but to wait until the plant reopens and probably would not be actively looking for work. However, it would be difficult to justify not classifying these workers as unemployed. Thus, the definition of unemployed persons was expanded to include certain groups, frequently termed the "inactive unemployed." These are persons who, although not actively looking for work in the specified week, report that they would have been doing so except for (1) their own temporary illness, (2) their belief that no work was available in their line of work or in the community, or (3) because they were awaiting recall to jobs from which they were on indefinite layoff.

Some modification of the "activity" concept was made also in the case of the employed. It was recognized that, if activity alone during a calendar week is considered, large numbers of persons who have definite job attachments but were temporarily absent from work in the survey week for reasons such as illness, vacation, or bad weather, would be excluded from the labor force count. Because, in most cases, their absence would not exceed a week or two, it was believed that their exclusion from the labor force would result in an unrealistic count of the economically active population. Moreover, unless looking for other jobs, they most logically belonged with the employed because they had jobs reserved for them in the economy. Thus, persons who were neither working nor looking for work but who had jobs or businesses from which they were temporarily absent during the survey week were set up as a separate group in the labor force. This group, "persons with jobs but not at work," is added to the "at work" group to derive estimates of the total number of employed persons.

There has been a good deal of discussion over the years concerning two very small components of the "with a job but not at work" group. These are persons who were not at work at their jobs because they are on temporary (less than 30-day) layoff, or because they were scheduled to report to new jobs within 30 days. Because these persons have less definite job attachments then others in the "with a job" category, and because their absence is usually involuntary, many believe they are more properly included with the unemployed. On the other hand, these persons presumably have jobs reserved for them and since they are not looking for other work and are not competing for jobs in the labor market, their status is different from that of persons who are completely jobless.

In any event, separate estimates of these two groups are published each month, and those who wish to regard them as unemployed or in some other class are thus able to do so. Over the past decade these two groups have not been numerically large, usually between 200,000 and 300,000 persons.

The classification as employed of persons working only a few hours in the survey week has also been the subject of much discussion. It has been suggested that when hours of work fall below a certain level (less than 15 hours, for example) these persons are more properly classified as partially unemployed. Information is provided in the Series P-57 report each month on hours worked by employed persons, so that the changes in the extent of full-time or part-time work can be readily observed. In addition, the quarterly studies of part-time workers show how many are working short hours because of economic factors and how many are doing so because they are housewives, students, or older persons who want, or are available for, only part-time employment.

The use of a fairly short period of reference (one week each month) imposes certain limitations on the interpretation of the data, particularly in trend analysis. Although the effects of factors such as adverse weather conditions, strikes, holidays, war situations, etc., are less marked in a one-week period than they would be if the time reference were shorter, say one day, they may nevertheless significantly influence the figures when they occur during the survey week. For example, unfavorable weather in some parts of the country may result in an apparent decline in farm employment in a given week as compared with the same period of the preceding year, although no significant economic change has actually taken place. Workers on strike may report themselves as looking for other employment, thereby increasing the unemployed total, although they will return to their old jobs when the dispute is settled. A legal holiday during the survey week is not likely to affect employment levels appreciably, but reported hours of work will decline. Such factors must, consequently, be taken into account in any interpretation and evaluation of the published figures.

In general, it is not possible to develop one or two over-all figures, such as the number of unemployed, that will be adequate to describe the whole complex of labor market phenomena. Consequently, the Current Population Survey is designed to provide a large amount of detailed and supplementary data which is available for use in interpreting and adjusting the broad totals to meet a wide variety of needs on the part of users of labor market information. The fact that this is a recurrent survey, however, operating under a tight time schedule, restricts the kinds of questions that may be asked. Many types of useful information, such as need for work, future job-seeking intentions, and reasons for present status, are less feasible in a recurrent than in a one-time survey.

Sources of errors in the survey estimates.--The estimates from the survey are subject to sampling errors, that is, errors arising from the fact that the estimates each month are based on information for only a relatively small sample instead of for all persons in the population. In addition, as in any survey work, the results are subject to errors in the field and to errors that occur in the processes of compilation.

Classification errors in labor force surveys may be particularly large in the case of persons with marginal attachments to the labor force. These errors may be caused by interviewers, respondents, or both, or may arise from faulty questionnaire design. The interviewers on the Current Population Survey are chiefly part-time workers. They are better trained than most field survey workers, having had repeated experience on this survey and having received a period of either direct or mail training each month prior to the survey. Moreover, thorough editing of their completed questionnaries, repeated observation during enumeration, and a systematic recheck of part of their assignments by the field supervisory staff, the work of the interviewers is kept under reasonable control and errors or deficiencies are brought directly to their attention.

In spite of these controls, interviewers may not always ask the questions in the prescribed fashion. To the extent that varying the wording of the questions results in differences in response, this factor may result in some errors or lack of uniformity in the statistics.

Similarly, the data are limited by the adequacy of the information possessed by the respondent and the willingness to report accurately. Usually, a single respondent, generally the housewife, reports for the entire family. The respondent may not know all the facts about family members or may be unable to report adequately on their attitudes or intentions. For example, the housewife will probably know that her husband is working, but she may not always know exactly how many hours he worked or the precise nature of his job.

The estimates from the survey are subject to various other types of errors beyond those already mentioned. Some of these are:

1. Nonresponse.--About 3 to 5 percent of occupied units are not interviewed in a typical month because of temporary absence of the occupants or various other reasons. Although an adjustment is made in weights for interviewed households to account for noninterviews, they still represent a possible source of bias. Similarly, for a relatively few interviewed households, some of the information is omitted because of lack of knowledge on the part of the respondent or because the interviewer forgot to ask certain questions or record the answers. In processing the questionnaires, entries are usually supplied for omitted items on the basis of the distributions in these items for persons of similar characteristics.

2. Independent population estimates.--The independent population estimates used in the estimation procedure (see discussion under "Ratio estimates," p. 6) may also provide a source of error, although on balance their use substantially improves the statistical reliability of many of the important figures. Errors may arise in the independent population estimates because of underenumeration of certain population groups or errors in age reporting in the last census (which serves as the base for the estimates) or similar problems in the components of population change (morbidity, immigration, etc.) since that date.

3. Processing errors.--Although there is a quality control program on coding and a close control on all other phases of processing and tabulation of the returns, some errors are almost inevitable in a substantial statistical operation of this type. It is likely, however, that the net error arising from processing is fairly negligible.

Measuring the accuracy of results.--Modern sampling theory provides methods for measuring the range of errors due to sampling where, as in the case of the Current Population Survey sample, the probability of selection of each member of the population is known. Methods are also available for measuring the effect of response variability in the Current Population Survey. A measure of sampling variability indicates the range of difference that may be expected due to the fact that only a sample of the population is surveyed. A measure of response variability indicates the range of difference that may be expected due to compensating types of errors arising from practices of different interviewers and the replies of respondents; these would tend to cancel out in an enumeration of a large enough population. In practice, these two sources of error--sampling and response variability, as defined above--are estimated jointly from the results of the survey. The computations do not, however, incorporate the effect of response bias, that is, any systematic errors of response such as those that would occur, if, by and large, respondents tended to overstate hours worked. Response biases occur in the same way in a complete census as in a sample, and, in fact, they may be smaller in a well-conducted sample survey because there it is feasible to pay the price necessary to collect the information more skillfully.

Estimates of sampling and response variability combined are provided in "The Monthly Report on the Labor Force" and in other reports based on the Current Population Survey, and the interpretation of data in the text of these reports is made in the light of the possible variability in the figures. In general, smaller figures and small differences between figures are subject to relatively large variation and should be interpreted with caution. The availability of the high-speed electronic computer will make it possible to provide considerably more detail on this subject in the future than has heretofore been possible.

The measurement of response bias is one of the most difficult aspects of survey and census work. Systematic studies on this subject are now an integral part of the Current Population Survey, but in many instances available techniques are not sufficiently precise to provide satisfactory estimates of the errors from response biases. A good deal of experimentation is in progress with the aim of developing more precise measurements and using the information to improve the over-all accuracy of the series.

COMPARABILITY WITH RELATED DATA

Household and establishment employment statistics.--Employment data published in "The Monthly Report on the Labor Force" (MRLF) are obtained by direct household interview and differ in some basic respects from related series based on reports from business establishments and farms. First, the household approach provides information on the work status of the entire population, without duplication, since each person is classified as employed, unemployed, or not in the labor force. Reports from nonagricultural establishments provide a payroll count, and consequently exclude persons who are not on a business payroll, such as proprietors, self-employed persons, unpaid family workers, and domestic servants. Persons who worked at more than one job during the survey week, however, are counted more than once in the establishment series but are classified in the job at which they worked the greatest number of hours in the MRLF series.

Second, the MRLF data refer to the week containing the eighth day of the month, whereas the payroll reports may refer to a different period in the month. Series that are subject to marked seasonal fluctuations may show different levels and changes in the two types of statistics because of the difference in timing of the surveys.

Third, only part of the "with a job but not at work" group, included in the MRLF employment total, appears on payrolls and would be counted in establishment reports. Persons on paid vacation or sick leave are included in both types of series. Workers on strike or temporary layoff during the survey week, however, are not on payrolls and would therefore not be counted in establishment statistics.

Finally, the MRLF and the current establishment statistics series are each subject to sampling variability and response errors, which may result in differences in both trends and levels.

Household unemployment series and unemployment insurance data.--The unemployment estimates published by the Bureau of the Census are not directly comparable with figures on unemployment compensation claims, although both series tend to show similar general trends. As in the case of employment data, unemployment figures obtained by household interview relate to the population as a whole. In contrast, large groups of workers are not covered by the unemployment insurance laws and are consequently not eligible for compensation. These groups include government workers, domestic servants, farm workers, the self-employed, and, in some States, employees of small enterprises.

Certain others who are looking for work are excluded from the claims figures because they are disqualified for benefits for various technical or administrative reasons or because they have exhausted their rights to compensation. Also excluded are new entrants in the labor market, who are definitely seeking work but have not been able to build up adequate wage credits through previous employment to entitle them to compensation.

On the other hand, certain persons who are eligible for unemployment insurance and have filed claims may not be classified as unemployed in the MRLF series. These would include some persons on temporary (less than 30-day) layoff from their jobs and some persons involuntarily working only a few hours who are eligible for partial benefits.

APPENDIX 6

Definitions and Classifications in the Measurement of Labor Force

A complete inventory of the economic status of our population calls for a count of those who work in a job, business or profession as well as of those who are not working, including information as to whether they are seeking work or not. The decennial census, based on a complete enumeration, can provide a mass of detail about the nation's manpower resources for individual localities by occupation and industry, age, sex, income, etc. The monthly survey, taken on a sample basis, obviously cannot provide the same quantity of detail or permit the same breakdown of information by localities as a census. However, in addition to information about the work activity of individuals during the survey period, it can furnish data on age and sex of those engaged in or looking for gainful activity, the number of hours spent at work or duration of unemployment and the major occupational and industrial characteristics of the population. The survey has also developed periodically other data that are descriptive of the economic characteristics of the population such as the extent of part-time employment and reasons for it, the educational and marital status of the working population, and work experience and income in the preceding year.

Classification of population in accordance with their economic activity presents numerous problems. When should a person be considered as working during a particular week of the month? All persons who do any gainful work, apart from housework or other work around the house or volunteer work, are treated, for the purpose of the monthly survey, as "at work." Similarly, persons who work on family farms or in a family business without pay are also considered "at work" if they spent at least 15 hours during the week in such activity (work for fewer weekly hours is disregarded as an "incidental" activity). Persons "at work" may also be looking for other employment, going to school, or giving even more time to doing their own housework. Some people "at work" may be working only part-time because of personal preference, others because no full-time work is available. Some work less than full-time hours because they started on their job in the midst of the survey week while others report shorter hours because their activity terminated during the week (as a matter of fact, as of the end of the week they may be either looking for other gainful work or else withdraw themselves from the employment market). When business is bad, some self-employed may spend full time at their work but suffer substantial reductions of income as a result of adverse economic conditions. Information on the number of hours spent at work during the survey week throws some light on the magnitude of short-time activity (although probably with a lesser degree of accuracy in the case of the self-employed). It fails, however, of itself, to indicate whether shorter hours are worked as a matter of personal choice or due to lack of sufficient work. Only by special inquiry can such information be elicited.

A somewhat different problem is presented by persons who did not work during the survey week although they actually had a job or a going business or profession at that time. The reasons, of course, differ. Some did not work because they were temporarily laid off with instructions to return to work within a comparatively short time (the Census Bureau uses a 30 day cut-off point for this purpose). Others may not have looked for work because they have already obtained a new job or got ready to start a new business subsequent to the survey week. It has been the practice of the Census Bureau to classify people in these circumstances as employed but not at work, and therefore to tally them as "employed" together with those who actually worked. There is a healthy disagreement about this practice and a number of experts feel that such persons "with a job but not at work" should more properly be classed with the unemployed, or else be segregated into a separate category distinct from either the employed or the unemployed. There is, of course, little doubt that the Census Bureau, by adding these groups in its employment totals and by not always showing them separately in its press releases, has unwittingly contributed to a certain amount of public misunderstanding of the data.

There are also other groups of individuals considered by the Census as with a job but not at work. They include people who had a job but were prevented from working by bad weather, those who fell sick while holding a job, who are on vacations from their jobs, who may not be working because of a labor dispute in their place of business and the like.

When is a person to be considered as unemployed? Not every one wants a job or an occupation. Some are too young to work -- the Census does not even attempt to obtain information on work activity of children under 14 years of age. Others may not seek work because they go to school, are retired or disabled, keep house or have independent income or for any other reason. To be meaningful, the unemployment status of a person must be related to his availability for gainful employment. The criterion used by the Census Bureau in classifying people as unemployed is that of a search for work while not working. As a rule, such information must be volunteered by the respondents. If other evidence of job search is volunteered during the interview -- registration with employment agencies in the past 60 days, writing of application letters, etc. -- such persons are also classed as unemployed even though no special effort to find work was made during the survey week. Similarly individuals are classified as unemployed if information is volunteered that they would have been seeking work except for a temporary illness or if they are waiting for a recall to a job from which they were laid off and if they believed that no employment was available in their line of work or in their community.

It is, of course, possible that some of the less articulate respondents may fail properly to indicate their unemployment status or that of other members of their household to the enumerators. For example, people drawing unemployment insurance and registered with public employment exchanges may not be counted as unemployed unless this information is volunteered by respondents. Some under-enumeration may also occur in the case of women who, in addition to their outside work, normally keep house or in case of individuals who are available only for part-time work. While such under-enumeration may be relatively small during periods of high employment, little is known about its extent during business down-swings. And yet, information on such groups may be highly significant in focusing attention on the trouble spots in the economy.

The mere fact of past employment is certainly not a criterion for present classification of a person as unemployed. Some people normally prefer to work intermittently -- during summer vacations in the case of students or at certain times of the year in case of certain seasonal occupations. At other times they may not seek work outside their own homes or the schools. On the other hand, when unemployment is severe, some individuals despairing to find jobs begin to look at themselves as unemployable and outside the labor market, and stop looking for work even though they are otherwise available for jobs. Under such circumstances, the present approach to measurement of unemployment may tend to understate its full extent. Nevertheless there may be some addition to the labor force at such times if the conditions induce several members of a family to search for work where only one of them previously worked.

The classifications of the population presently used by the Census Bureau have remained substantially unchanged ever since the monthly survey was begun in 1940 under WPA auspices. There is need for a thorough re-examination of them. This was noted, for example, in the Report of Panel on Census Statistics on the Labor Force to the Intensive Review Committee. (See Appendix 3.) The Panel urged, for example, that the work status of the labor force is not adequately described by a simple division into the employed and the unemployed and urged increased study of definitions and concepts aimed at a greater clarification of the several areas of uncertainty provided by the present classifications. It has also pointed out the need for further refinements needed in definitions and tabulations to insure greater usefulness of the labor force information for many analytical uses.

The Committee is in full accord with the recommendations of the Panel on the Labor Force. It realizes, of course, that many of such improvements, particularly those which call for finer classifications of data, are dependent on the enlargement of the present sample size. It is also conscious of the fact that there is a definite need for creating better public understanding of labor force measurement. One present source of public confusion arises, for example, because frequently the users of labor force statistics mistakenly treat the term "employment" as including only persons who stand in the relation of an employee to an employer. The creation of an intermediate category, such as that recommended by the Labor Force Panel, comprising persons with jobs or businesses but not at work, would eliminate the need of using the term "employment" with regard to those "at work". This term might be used as a basis for a classification scheme along the following lines:

(1) At work
(2) Not working, with a job
(3) Not working, with a business
(4) Not working, looking for work
(5) Not working, not looking for work

The actual task of developing the revised concepts and classification is a long-range undertaking beyond the resources commanded by the present Committee. For this reason we commend this problem to the review committee on the labor force, as recommended elsewhere in this report.

There are many other problems of definition and classification that must be investigated and solved. For example, there is at any one time a certain number of individuals and families that are on the move, relocating from one place to another. While they are travelling and perhaps even for a somewhat longer period they are not likely to be included in the enumeration of the sample segments. Thus, the enumerator may record a given dwelling unit as unoccupied at the time of his visit in the enumeration week because one household has just moved out and its successors have not yet moved in. Family units are especially likely to be missed when they are in transit relocating from one section of the country to another. The exact size of these groups and their labor force status are not known. Yet, by special studies made periodically of the occupants of dwelling units, it should be possible to obtain information on their whereabouts and status during the enumeration period of the preceding month and thus estimate the number and characteristics of people who were omitted in the previous month's survey. Other techniques can also be developed. This is but one of several problems that arise from the practical impossibility of interviewing all the people in the sample and of giving full representation in the sample to persons who are not living in a dwelling during some or all of the survey period. Another set of problems is presented by the population in the Armed Forces and by the population in institutions of various kinds. In the aggregate these problems are important and should be included in a program of long-range inquiries.

APPENDIX 7

Questionnaire and Interview

Several factors can affect the count of those in the labor force. Some of them relate to the nature of the basic concepts--who is to be included in the labor force and how different individuals are to be classified within it. Other factors relate to the collection of information--the type of questions asked of the respondents, the enumerators' understanding of their instructions, the manner in which they approach the task of the interview, the understanding by the respondents of the questions asked, and their willingness and ability to provide the desired information.

The fundamental concepts and definitions that establish the various categories into which the labor force is divided by the Census in the Current Population Survey are not as simple or as easily ascertainable as some of the questions usually asked in other Census surveys. They are not as definite and clear-cut, for example, as the questions on sex, age, or marital status. The information that is needed for an accurate count and correct classification of persons in the various categories of the labor force must, therefore, be obtained not by a single question but by a series of questions. In specific instances, no questionnaire can list all of these beforehand; some may have to be formulated on the spot to meet the particular situation of the person that is being questioned. It is essential, however, that whatever questions are asked, they be so phrased as to bring out the real status of individuals in the labor force. Data so gathered by all interviewers must be strictly comparable and in agreement with the basic concepts of the enumeration. Only in this way can the results of the interviews be properly combined into meaningful and accurate totals. The interview, of course, must be conducted in a relatively brief period in the homes of the respondents without placing an unreasonable burden on their patience and cooperativeness. The number of questions may also have to be limited on account of costs. This, of course, precludes as much questioning as might otherwise be desirable.

The Census Bureau is caught in a dilemma. On the one hand, it must obtain sufficient information to make correct classifications of individuals into the labor force categories. On the other hand, it is under strong pressures to make interviewing relatively simple and brief and to keep expenditures within budgetary limits. It must also meet the standards of statistical quality which are rightfully demanded of it. And at the same time, it must attempt to observe the practical rules and principles that are commonly accepted as essential to success in periodic surveys. The Committee feels that while the Bureau has done exceptionally well in attempting to reconcile the many conflicting demands, it still can and should make substantial improvements in the questionnaire, instructions and other interviewing procedures in the labor force field.

The accomplishment of these improvements must come, in large measure, from thoroughgoing studies and tests of interviewing procedures, but also in part from ingenuity and application of certain widely recognized principles derived from the existing body of survey experience to which the Census Bureau has itself contributed so much. Some of these are:

1. Instructions for the interviewers should be relatively simple and brief with major guidance to the interviewer provided by the questions themselves.

2. The questions should be so phrased as to make them readily understandable to the respondents and avoid incorrect responses that follow misunderstanding of the questions. They should not provoke resistance on the part of the respondents which would manifest itself in unwillingness to answer or to be interviewed several times or which would induce respondents to provide inaccurate or misleading answers.

3. Each question should be narrowed down to a specific issue and call for a responsible answer within a specific framework of reference.

4. The questionnaire should elicit sufficient basic information to enable supervisors and others to determine, from the responses secured in the field, the appropriate classification to be made. Interviewers should not be required to perform complex classification and coding or to "edit" the questionnaire for internal consistency. The interviewer should have an absolute minimum of need to depart from the printed questions or explanations in the course of the interview. Every question asked which is properly required to establish an individual's classification should be recorded rather than the final conclusions which were drawn from a series of questions.

5. The questionnaire should provide a logical development of questions and should not require interviewers to go back to correct the previously given answers (except in the isolated case when the respondent himself draws the interviewer's attention to a misstatement previously made in the course of the interview).

6. The questions must deal with matters which can normally be expected to be within the knowledge of responsible respondents.

7. In order to minimize error, the questionnaire should be printed in a form primarily designed for the convenience of conducting the interview. It should be in sufficiently large and readable type and allow sufficient space for recording answers and comments, particularly when these do not conform to the standard classification given on the forms.

The Census Bureau, is, of course, fully conversant with these requirements. However, costs and other practical considerations do not always permit adherence to these principles.

Two basic types of questionnaires are presently used by the Census enumerators in the course of interviewing. The first of these is the Field Control Card (Form 1610-e, see page A-47). It is filled out in the course of the initial interview in a given household. At that time the names of all persons residing in the household are listed on this form together with several items of demographic information--the relationship of the several individuals to the head of the household, their marital status, age, sex and race as well as their veteran or military service status. In addition, the type of dwelling occupied by the household is noted on the card as well as the information as to whether subsequent interviews may be conducted by phone. The schedule also contains room for notation of subsequent visits. At such times the interviewer is supposed to recheck to determine whether there were any changes in the household composition and make appropriate entries on the card. Failure to make changes, however, is not self-evident from the card. The interviewer carries the card, as originally filled out and subsequently modified, at all visits to the same household.

The second questionnaire (Form 1605C, see Pages A-48 and A-49) is used to record the information about the labor force status of each individual in the household who is 14 years of age or over. Originally, information about all members of the household was recorded on a single form (unless the size of the household was such that more than one sheet was required). At the present time, a separate card is used for each such member of the household. In part it carries information about the individual which links him to the Field Control Card; this is recorded on one face of the card. On the reverse side, answers are entered about the current labor force status of the individual. There are 10 standard questions in this regard. Periodically, however, questions are added to cover additional aspects of the labor force participation and for other purposes. The standard questionnaire, printed in very small type, is compressed in a very small space, approximately 7 by 3 inches. In case of eight out of the ten standard questions, the interviewer is required to record the answers by mark-sensing, i.e. by making strokes with a special pencil in the appropriate spaces provided for the answers. The card then can be handled mechanically for the purpose of final tabulations.

The present questionnaire for the labor force interviews is highly skeletonized. The interviewer cannot, therefore, always rely on the questions printed on the schedule. In such cases, the interviewer has to rephrase and elaborate the printed questions, in accordance with the instructions provided by the Enumerator's Manual in order to obtain proper responses. In these circumstances, unconsciously, the interviewer may inject his own personality into the questioning to a much greater degree than seems desirable for objective reporting, by the phrasing of additional questions, by the choice of questions and by the degree of precision with which such extra information is elicited. However, the existing schedule provides no record of any such additional questions asked. It is in effect merely a statement of conclusions reached as a result of the questions that happen to be asked. Many questions do, of course, evoke an immediate response without supplementary probing. In some situations, however, the responses may actually provide inaccurate data although the available information on the schedule may be inadequate to establish this.

It is, of course, most desirable for the questionnaire to be self-checking. This would enable the editors in a central or a field office, on the basis of the information elicited from the respondents and without any modification of responses by the interviewers, to obtain the true picture of the individual's status in the labor force.

The task of designing a questionnaire is a complex undertaking and is clearly not within the scope or the resources of this Committee to carry out. All the Committee hopes to do is to show, by means of several illustrations below, some of the shortcomings of the existing schedules in order to highlight the need for revision.

A shortcoming in the design of the questionnaire is demonstrated, for example, by what appears to be an unusual clustering of responses at 40 hours of work per week. It is quite likely that many respondents misconstrue the question on the number of hours "worked last week." Thus instead of giving the number of hours a particular individual _actually_ worked, they provide information on the number of hours _normally_ worked. There is no reason for such a misunderstanding since the problem, encountered in interviewing outside the Census Bureau, has been basically overcome by resort to two questions instead of one, the first of these clarifying the second. In case of hours of work, the first such question could well inquire about the number of hours a given individual normally works per week. The second question would then call for the number of hours the individual has actually worked last week. The purpose of this technique is to draw the attention of the respondent to the specific technical meaning of the question and thus help to improve the accuracy of information.

So long as the questioning of respondents was conducted in the course of a single week for the week for which information was sought, the phrasing of questions in terms of the happenings of "last week" was adequate. Under the current procedures, however, the interviewing of respondents extends over a period longer than a calendar week. The question as phrased is prone, therefore, to secure incorrect information. Thus when respondents will be interviewed during the second enumeration week, they will talk about the week of the 15th of the month rather than that of the 8th.

The length of the period of unemployment, obtained by inquiring about the number of weeks the individual has been looking for work, raises a question: as of what date? The information is sought, of course, as of the week of the 8th of the month. But from the way the question is phrased, it appears probable that responses will portray the situation as of the time the interviews are taking place.

Another problem in this connection is highlighted by the instructions contained in the Enumerator's Manual regarding the concept of the period during which an individual was looking for work:

> In computing the length of time a person has been looking for work, count the number of weeks from the time he started looking for work through the end of the survey week for the current month.
>
> However, if it is indicated that an interruption has occurred in the period of looking for work, the number of weeks entered here should represent the present continuous period of looking for work.

> In this connection a period of 2 weeks or more during which a person was employed or ceased looking for work . . . is considered to break the continuity of the present period of seeking work. In such cases, enter the number of weeks of the present period of looking for work, counting from the end of the "break in continuity" through the end of the survey week. (Enumerator's Manual, p. 159.)

As a matter of actual fact, the schedules used by interviewers supplies them with the following question to be asked during the interview: "How many weeks has . . . been looking for work?" The respondent is clearly unaware of the narrow meanings given to the term "how many weeks" by the Census instructions. For that matter, as the above citation makes clear, only when "it is indicated" in the course of an interview that "breaks in continuity" have occurred during the period of search for work, will the latest spell of continuous search be considered. Reliance is thus placed, in the first instance, on casual remarks uttered in the course of the interview, and in the second instance, on the interviewer continuing the questioning for details in the absence of specific instructions to do so. (A similar problem of modification of the question, depending on the respondent's casual remarks, occurs in connection with the treatment of "looking for work" replies.) This question illustrates the type of difficulty which arises unavoidably when information is sought within a single query when as a matter of fact, several formalized questions are necessary to elicit the facts.

While the intent of the present questionnaire is, at least in part, to enable the Census to obtain information on the employment status of the respondent or of members of his household in more than one way, the questionnaire fails to do so without injecting, to an inordinate degree, the personal judgment of the interviewers necessitated by departures from the formal questions on the schedule. This occurs beginning with the very first question on the labor force: "What was . . . doing most of last week, working, keeping house, going to school or something else?" In the case of certain responses this question cannot be handled without further elaboration. This is particularly true in the case of possible situations which call for classification of individuals as "With a job but not at work" or "Unable to work." Actually, such answers are not responses to the question asked, particularly in the case of the first of these classifications. The question calls for data on activity, and not status. Thus an individual is most likely to be described as "not working," "staying at home," "being ill or disabled" rather than in the form suitable for entry on the existing questionnaire. The schedule, in fact, lists conclusions which can only be drawn after additional information is first secured. Thus an individual who indicates that some one was not working last week, will have to be asked "why?" The answers to this may be "sick," "could not work," "could not work because of accident or sickness," "was laid off," "was laid off for a week," "don't have to work," "taking a vacation," "wanted to go fishing," and so on. In case of sickness additional information is required about its permanent or temporary character in order to permit the final classification of the individual as "unable to work," in the technical meaning of this term as given to it by the Census Bureau, but not before. Yet, the present schedule treats this condition in the form of a single entry, based on data (if any were obtained in the course of the interview) that remain solely a private matter between the respondent and interviewer. The regional or central office can in no way determine the accuracy or the propriety of such classification without a revisit to the household. Yet, the details available to the interviewer for classification purposes should also be available to central authorities of the Census for proper editing and check on accuracy of the response. The same is also true of the "with a job and not at work" category, although probably to a lesser degree since additional questions about this status are called for by the existing schedules. In the case of the "unable to work" group, however, no further information is sought beyond the initial question.

There are, of course, many other problems which arise in the construction of a proper questionnaire. This Committee can only indicate some of the fundamental issues involved which need additional study and experimentation. What is true about providing a sound design for the taking of the survey, is equally true for the development of the questionnaire, the sequence of questions asked and their framework of reference. For example, in the case of supplementary questions addressed to persons who worked less than 35 hours during the survey week regarding their typical work patterns, it would appear more reasonable to bring such questions immediately after the respondents are asked the initial questions on working hours, rather than at the end of the basic interview.

It is also important to ensure that the information obtained be meaningful in the light of the phenomenon it is supposed to measure. Unless this is done, the statistics may be of doubtful validity. For example, in May 1954 supplementary questions were asked of persons looking for work regarding their receipt of unemployment insurance. The figures obtained in the course of enumeration, however, cannot be properly related to other figures in the overall national picture. The Census concept of who is "unemployed" during the week differs from that under the unemployment insurance laws. For example, a part-time worker who worked a fraction of his usual time during the survey week may be legally entitled to receive unemployment insurance for part-total or partial unemployment. The Census, however, treats such persons as "at work" during the week and hence not as "unemployed." Thus the totals produced by the Census survey could not match the totals of workers receiving unemployment insurance during the survey week. Thus it is very doubtful whether figures collected in such an enumeration will describe a group of the labor force that is readily understood by the public.

There is, of course, another question at issue: How much do the respondents to the enumeration--who, in many instances, are not the persons about whom the information is sought--know about the status of individual members of their households with regard to unemployment insurance? In some cases, they undoubtedly would and in other situations not. For that matter, the circumstances surrounding the receipt of unemployment insurance benefits help to confuse the issue. Some individuals may not receive benefits simply because, for one reason or another, they are not eligible or entitled to such benefits. On the other hand a number of individuals, who qualify under the state statutes to receive benefits, may not have received them as of the time of the interview, either because the survey week coincided with their legally-required waiting (non-compensable) period or because of the delay in payments. This example illustrates the need for extreme care in designing additional questions to get meaningful data.

The proper design of the questions is particularly important if supervision is to be effectively utilized to insure the essential accuracy of the results. In one sense this calls for self-checking interviews which would enable supervisors and others to determine, from the raw material obtained in the field by the way of responses, whether or not appropriate classifications have been made. On the other hand, if the primary check of the questionnaires, in the course of editing, is to be the conformity of the responses to given patterns, then the supervisory personnel is in no position to determine whether the information secured in the field is accurate in fact or whether it was merely made "to fit" by the editorial efforts of the interviewers.

The needed revision of the existing questionnaires is a task of major magnitude. This subject properly falls within the scope of the review committee, the creation of which is recommended by the Committee elsewhere in this report.

Appendix 7

CURRENT POPULATION SURVEY FIELD CONTROL CARD

CONFIDENTIAL - This inquiry is authorized by Section 1 (b), Public Law 671 of the 80th Congress (62 Stat. 478, 13 U.S.C., 121-123). This Census Report is CONFIDENTIAL and cannot be used for purposes of taxation, investigation, or regulation.

Form P-1610a (6-9-54)

U.S. DEPARTMENT OF COMMERCE
BUREAU OF THE CENSUS

CURRENT POPULATION SURVEY - FIELD CONTROL CARD

1. IDEN. CODE | 2. DISTRICT SEGMENT NO. | 3. SAMPLE A - 4 | 4. HOUSEHOLD NO.

BUDGET BUREAU NO. 41-R1201.1
APPROVAL EXPIRES NOVEMBER 30, 1954

5. BLOCK OR RURAL SAMPLE AREA
6. SAMPLE AREA
7. STATE

8. CONTROL NO.

9. ADDRESS (Enter house number and st., apt. number, and other identification)

and

☐ Farm Bldgs.
☐ Store
☐ Garage
☐ Other (Specify)

9a. MAILING ADDRESS (If different from above)

10. Was a "Dear Friend" letter sent in advance of first enumeration?
☐ Yes ☐ No

11. LOCATION OF UNIT
Is this house on a farm (or ranch)?
☐ Yes ☐ No

12. TYPE OF LIVING QUARTERS
☐ DWELLING UNIT - House, apartment, flat, trailer, tent, cabin in tourist court mainly for PERMANENT guests, etc.
☐ OTHER - Room(s) not a dwelling unit in a hotel, lodginghouse, cabin in tourist court mainly for TRANSIENT guests, etc.

Line No.	NAME (Last name first) List all persons staying here and all persons who usually live here who are absent. Be sure to include infants under 1 year of age.	RELATIONSHIP TO HEAD OF HOUSEHOLD (Enter head, wife, son, daughter-in-law, partner, lodger, lodger's wife, etc.)	HOUSEHOLD MEMBER (Yes or No)	FOR PERSONS WITH YES IN 16: MARITAL STATUS (M, Wd, D, Sep or NM)	DATE OF BIRTH (Enter in numerals) Month	Day	Year	AGE: Enter age as of last birthday. If under 1 year, enter "0."			AGE: Month and year of age change. (In numerals)		RACE (W Neg. or OT)	SEX (M or F)	VETERAN STATUS OF MALES 14 YRS. OF AGE & OVER: Did ... ever serve for any time at all in the armed forces of the U.S.? (Yes or No)	If YES in 22a Was this service during World War II?* (Yes or No)	Enter AF if now in the armed forces	CHANGES IN HOUSEHOLD COMPOSITION
(13)	(14)	(15)	(16)	(17)	(18a)	(18b)	(18c)	(19a)	(19b)	(19c)	(19d)	(19e)	(20)	(21)	(22a)	(22b)	(23)	(24)
1																		
2																		
3																		
4																		
5																		
6																		
7																		
8																		
9																		
10																		

25. CHECK OF HOUSEHOLD COMPOSITION
a. (Ask each month) We have now listed ..., is there anyone else staying here? ⟶ Yes / No
b. (Ask first month only) - Have we missed anyone who is away -
on business? ☐ Yes ☐ No
at school? ☐ Yes ☐ No
on a vacation? ☐ Yes ☐ No
on a visit? ☐ Yes ☐ No
temporarily in a hospital? ☐ Yes ☐ No

Yes	No	Month and year (Example: 10/54)	26. NO. OF VISITS, NONINTERVIEW REASON, AND NOTES: Tally of visits	Noninterview reason	Notes (On callbacks, etc.)

(Continue Notes on back)

* September 16, 1940 - July 25, 1947

27. USE OF TELEPHONE:
a. Does unit have a telephone? ☐ Yes ☐ No
Number: ____________
b. If "Yes," in (a), is telephone interview acceptable? ☐ Yes ☐ No

28. TIME TO VISIT:

29.

Comm-DC 27197

CURRENT POPULATION SURVEY LABOR-FORCE QUESTIONNAIRE - FRONT

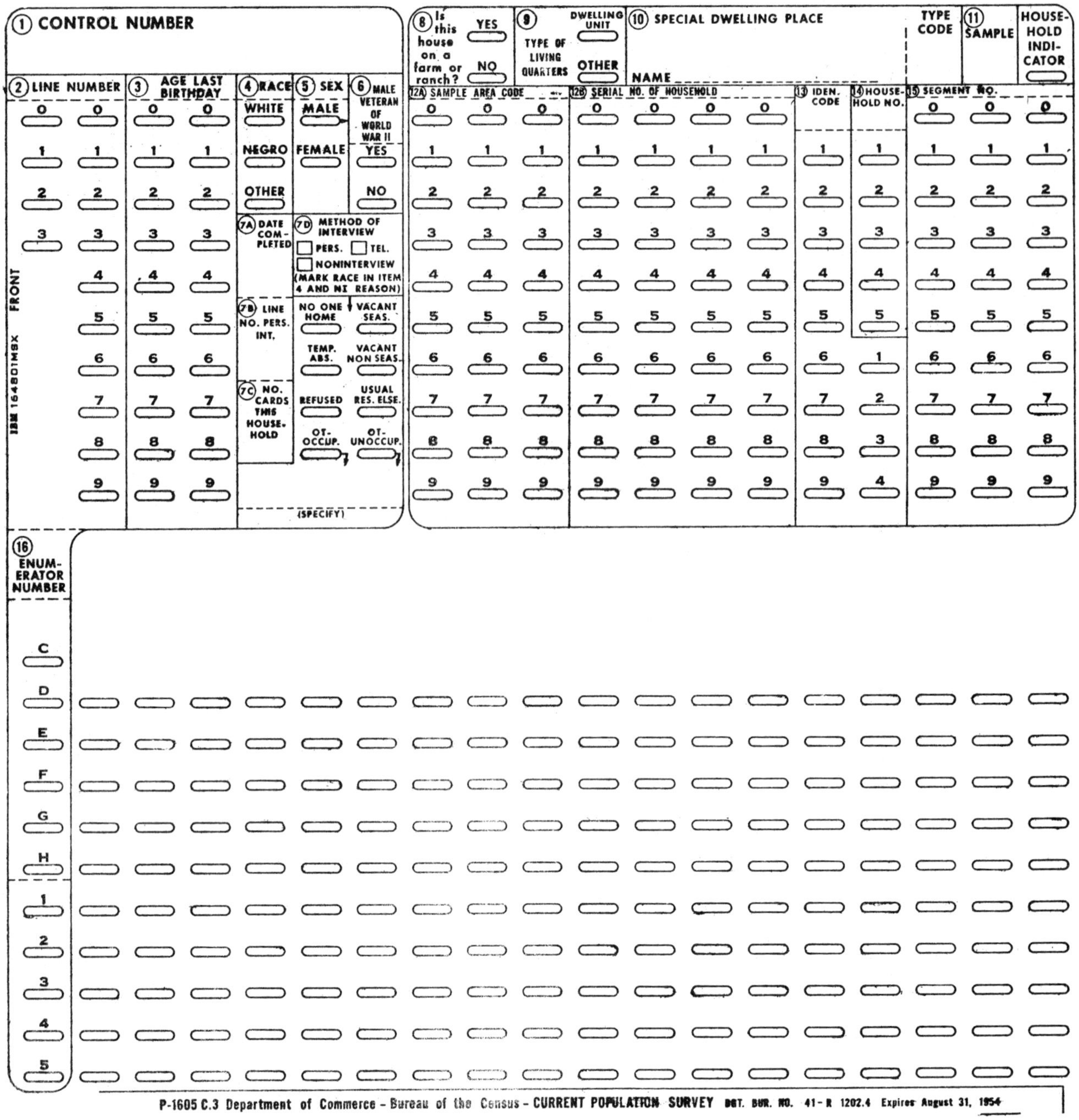

(1) CONTROL NUMBER

(2) LINE NUMBER
(3) AGE LAST BIRTHDAY
(4) RACE: WHITE, NEGRO, OTHER
(5) SEX: MALE, FEMALE
(6) MALE VETERAN OF WORLD WAR II: YES, NO
(7A) DATE COMPLETED
(7B) LINE NO. PERS. INT.
(7C) NO. CARDS THIS HOUSEHOLD
(7D) METHOD OF INTERVIEW: PERS. TEL. NONINTERVIEW (MARK RACE IN ITEM 4 AND NI REASON)
NO ONE HOME; VACANT SEAS.; TEMP. ABS.; VACANT NON SEAS.; REFUSED; USUAL RES. ELSE.; OT-OCCUP.; OT-UNOCCUP.
(SPECIFY)

(8) Is this house on a farm or ranch? YES NO
(9) TYPE OF LIVING QUARTERS: DWELLING UNIT, OTHER
(10) SPECIAL DWELLING PLACE: NAME
TYPE CODE
(11) SAMPLE
HOUSEHOLD INDICATOR
(12A) SAMPLE AREA CODE
(12B) SERIAL NO. OF HOUSEHOLD
(13) IDEN. CODE
(14) HOUSEHOLD NO.
(15) SEGMENT NO.

(16) ENUMERATOR NUMBER: C D E F G H 1 2 3 4 5

IBM 164801MSX FRONT

P-1605 C.3 Department of Commerce - Bureau of the Census - CURRENT POPULATION SURVEY BGT. BUR. NO. 41-R 1202.4 Expires August 31, 1954

CURRENT POPULATION SURVEY LABOR-FORCE QUESTIONNAIRE - BACK

FILL 18-26 FOR CIVILIAN HOUSEHOLD MEMBERS 14 YEARS OLD & OVER

(18) LINE NO. OF THIS PERSON

(19) What was . . . doing most of last week-
- Working
- Keeping house
- Going to school

Or something else?

WORKING (Skip to 21)	WK→
LOOKING FOR WORK	LK
WITH A JOB BUT NOT AT WORK	J
KEEPING HOUSE	H
GOING TO SCHOOL	S
UNABLE TO WORK (Omit 20-26)	U
OTHER (Specify) ↓	OT

(20) Did . . . do any work at all last week, not counting work around the house?
YES (WK) NO (Ask 22)→

(21) How many hours did . . . work last week?
0 0 / 1 1 / 2 2 / 3 3 / 4 4 / 5 5 / 6 6 / 7 7 / 8 8 / 9 9
(Skip to Item 26, and enter job worked at last week)

(22) (If LK in 19, skip to 23) Was . . . looking for work? (Include special cases)
YES (LK) NO (Ask 24)→

(23) How many weeks has . . . been looking for work?
0 0 / 1 1 / 2 2 / 3 3 / 4 4 / 5 5 / 6 6 / 7 7 / 8 8 / 9 9
(Skip to Item 26, and enter last full-time civilian job)

(24) (If J in 19, skip to 25) Even though . . . did not work last week, does he have a job or business?
YES (J) NO (Omit 25 & 26)

(25) Why was . . . absent from work last week?
- OWN ILLNESS
- ON VACATION
- BAD WEATHER
- LABOR DISPUTE
- TEMPORARY LAYOFF (less than 30 days)
- NEW JOB TO BEGIN WITHIN 30 DAYS
- OTHER (Specify) ↓

(Skip to Item 26, and enter job held last week)

(17) CONTROL NO.

(26) DESCRIPTION OF JOB OR BUSINESS

A. OCCUPATION - What kind of work was . . . doing? (For example: civil engineer, stock clerk, typist, farmer, etc.)

B. INDUSTRY - What kind of business or industry was . . . working in? (For example: radio factory, retail shoe store, State labor department, farm, etc.)

C. CLASS OF WORKER

For PRIVATE employer for wages, salary, commission or tips	P
For GOVERNMENT (Federal, State, local, etc.)	G
In OWN business, profession or farm for profit or fees	O
WITHOUT PAY on family farm or business	NP
NEVER WORKED	NEV

IBM 157414MSX BACK

FOR OFFICE USE ONLY

(A)	(B)	
VV	V	V
70	X	X
00	0	0
11	1	1
22	2	2
33	3	3
44	4	4
55	5	5
66	6	6
77	7	7
88	8	8
99	9	9

APPENDIX 8

Control and Quality Checks of Survey Procedures

The attainment and maintenance of high quality interviewing is a complex and difficult task. Considerable resources of the Census Bureau have been devoted to this purpose in the past and even greater expenditures of time and funds will be required in the future. The problem is equally important and difficult in the work of other governmental and non-governmental organizations that undertake statistical survey work. It is all to the credit of governmental agencies that they pay considerable attention to this problem. This must be emphasized because the greater the effort expended in quality tests, the greater the number of defects that will be discovered. Only if they are discovered can they be taken into account and corrected. Surveys that are not thoroughly checked for accuracy provide a false impression of high quality that they do not possess. It is ironical that they often escape criticism while they mislead or deceive the people who use them.

To insure a high quality of interviewing it is, of course, essential to determine and to test the effectiveness of all phases of interviewer operations. The variety of tests, whether formal or informal in nature, must supplement each other effectively, for no type of test by itself can guarantee the effective conduct of the survey work. Adequate supervision is just as necessary as the more mechanical tests of individual or group performance by interviewers.

In the case of the Census Bureau, quality controls begin, in effect, at the time interviewers are first selected as suitable for their future assignment, and thereafter trained in the techniques of interviewing and in the basic concepts and procedures of the survey. They are continued through on-the-job training, both in the early stages of visits by new enumerators when they are accompanied by supervisors, through follow-up training material and tests periodically taken by all interviewers, by means of group or individual meetings between interviewers and their supervisors devoted to the discussion of problems encountered in the field, as well as additional follow-ups of work of individual interviewers who seem to need additional assistance and checking of their work. In addition, controls over the quality of interviewing consist of rechecks of work of individual interviewers to determine the degree of accuracy of the survey work and of the responses secured in the course of the interviews as well as to determine the character of performance of individual interviewers.

While all potential enumerators are given a test to determine their suitability for the work, an administrative problem has been created when, beginning with the spring months of 1953, regional offices of the Census Bureau were instructed to employ enumerators only through the recommendations of local political organizations of the party in power (unless local leadership has indicated in writing that they are not in a position to recommend any candidates for the job). This has created several difficulties on the local level. The needed replacements of staff could not always be obtained promptly; yet, it appears, that no local political leader wanted to go on record as unable to supply the needed personnel. Admittedly for this and many other reasons, this is not the most effective and desirable system of recruiting. Commenting on a similar problem in connection with the decennial census enumerations, where a long standing tradition was to recruit personnel through political organizations, the Intensive Review Committee appraising Census programs, noted: "With the creation and development of the State Employment Services and the United States Employment Service, and the development of methods and techniques for recruiting and training, there can no longer be any justification for resort to those outmoded procedures" and recommended: "That appropriate steps be taken to assure the recruiting and training of qualified field supervisors and enumerators for the 1960 census through substituting for political nomination the sole test of qualification". Clearly, a similar procedure should be followed in the recruiting of field enumeration staff for the current surveys. The value of these positions, which are at best on a part-time basis, is too small to mean much to the political organizations. The loss of efficiency which the present procedure entails, however, in the recruitment of personnel may be great.

The training of new enumerators is a time-consuming undertaking for supervisors, particularly since in many small areas which are being sampled there is usually but a single enumerator. In the first instance, the supervisor is required to spend approximately two days with the new interviewer going over the manual of procedure with him and explaining operating problems by means of mock interviews. Thereafter, the recruit spends four hours in home study, reading assignments from working manuals and completing review exercises which are then mailed to the supervisor. Finally, at the time of the first week of actual interviews, the supervisor is scheduled to spend about a day with the new interviewer, preferably one or two days after he began interviewing. During the second month on the job (about two weeks before the enumeration), the interviewer is mailed additional home study materials and exercises for which he is allowed about four hours of paid study time and the supervisor is scheduled to spend another day with the interviewer sometime during the enumeration week for additional observation and discussion of problems. Finally, during the third month on the job, additional study and exercise materials are mailed to the enumerator; about three paid hours is allowed for this study. Instead of visiting the enumerator during the survey week, the supervisor is expected to phone him after review of completed homework to point out errors or any misunderstandings which were exhibited by the exercises, or else the interviewers, when feasible, may come to the supervisor's office for this purpose. Thereafter personal contacts between the supervisor and the interviewer are put on a much more infrequent time schedule, with supervisors scheduled to visit enumerators in areas away from their office about three times a year. However, follow-up instructions and exercise materials are regularly mailed to interviewers in an effort to maintain their training. In the past, it has been customary in all areas to hold regular monthly or bi-monthly group training sessions with interviewers. Under the present organizational plan there is, however, no provision for the continuation of this practice on a regular basis. The future will, undoubtedly, throw light on the wisdom of this policy.

An observation needs to be made in this connection about the unquestioned complexity and difficulty of the labor force surveys -- they are among the more arduous which must be undertaken by the Federal Government. This is evident even in the very size of the Enumerator's Manual -- a 240 page volume with 144 pages devoted solely to the problems of enumeration. The continued need to expand this document in order to take into account the many questions that had to be resolved over a period of years is further illustrated by the fact that in 1945 the enumerating instructions required only 36 pages of text. Thus the quality of enumerator's work must clearly depend very greatly on the quality of the instruction he receives, the nature of the refresher training and the competence and proximity of supervision.

However, these measures are not sufficient, by themselves, to insure high quality of enumeration. Moreover, resources are not always available to accomplish fully the specified procedures. Individual interviewers of necessity operate on their own most of the time. Their conversations with respondents, as summarized on the schedules, may appear to be consistent and yet may unwittingly conceal inaccuracies which could be detected only if the errors were made in the presence of supervisors or if they were uncovered by a recheck with the respondents. The problem is particularly acute when supervision is actually removed from the immediate areas where enumeration is conducted and when the enumeration in many sections of the country is dependent on the work of a single interviewer whose understanding of the problems involved in enumeration is subject to many natural human errors and biases.

There is thus a definite need to institute quality checks over the work of interviewers. At the present time the Bureau of the Census utilizes several different controls for this purpose. Records are maintained of the ratio of errors made by individual interviewers that are detected in the process of editing the completed schedules. On the basis of such records, it is possible to indicate to the enumerators where they need to improve their performance. In addition, a mail follow-up of interviewing is carried on for a modest number of the households that were interviewed by each enumerator in a given month. The replies obtained from respondents who answer the Census letter provide an indication of gross mistakes and serve as a check that the households have actually been visited by the enumerators. However, many respondents suffer from lapses of memories, and substantial numbers even fail to return the questionnaire. Thus, the usefulness of this device is somewhat limited. Furthermore, in view of the difficulties of assessing the characteristics of those respondents who fail to reply, it is impossible to establish statistically valid criteria for evaluating any of the results of the survey. The relative cheapness of this method of follow-up suggests, however, that it may be a useful disciplinary measure to keep interviewers on their toes, as it would usually bring to light promptly any extensive falsification of reports.

A much more useful device presently employed by the Census Bureau is an actual recheck based on second visits to the households following the completion of the original interview. At the present time a random and clustered subsample of about two percent of the enumerated households is visited by supervisors for this purpose. This seems to be a promising method for determining the quality of the original interviews. However, this method, at the present, fails to bring to light inaccuracies which are common to all interviewing because it is limited to much too small a part of the total sample. Reliable results based on these enumerations must, therefore, wait until recheck data are accumulated over a considerable period of time. Thus recheck procedures seem to offer but a sluggish indicator of the sources of inaccuracy that need correction. Although this method does reveal specific types of discrepancies, it does not always indicate the specific nature of the errors or the way in which they should be corrected. Yet, despite the present limitations, the recheck by personal visits is an exceedingly useful device which calls for further development along several lines. On the one hand, it can be used to compare the results obtained in the course of the revisit with those secured in the original interview with a view to discussions with interviewers as to the possible causes of discrepancies when such occur. This has already been initiated by the Census Bureau. Secondly, the enlargement of the sample of reinterviews and the follow-up of the interviews taken by individual interviewers in a systematic fashion in order to determine the degree of accuracy achieved by them may serve to become an excellent control device of the performance of individual interviewers. Sequential sampling of the results obtained by individual interviewers should enable the Census Bureau to develop objective standards of interviewer performance, suitable both for corrective and disciplinary actions. They should be planned in a way to insure that every interviewer is checked in this fashion at least once in the course of a calendar year. While at the present time checking is done by local supervisors, it is possible that the development of a central control personnel, operating directly out of Washington, may bring about a better degree of control over such work. Thirdly, the random sampling of the original interviews for recheck purposes may permit a broad view of the comparative accuracy of results.

The quality control of interviewing is a major task of the Census and one for which additional measures for controlling quality have to be developed and tried experimentally. The development of these measures and further considerations of ways and means of achieving and maintaining an adequate degree of accuracy should be one of the major areas for future research and one with which the proposed review committee may well be concerned.

APPENDIX 9

Interviewer Production Quotas

In the execution of any large scale survey where individuals perform more or less independently, it is necessary to have some form of control over the quality and quantity of performance. The Census Bureau has recognized this need and over a course of years from 1942 until the present such controls have been developed. The Census aims at obtaining maximum performance at a given standard of quality. It has developed production quotas by observing the performance of individual interviewers. For those interviewers where the performance is below the range of acceptable quantity, supervisors have looked into the situation; in some cases, they have suggested remedial action, and in other cases they have discharged the interviewers. By examining the details of performance among those interviewers whose quantity has appeared above average, supervisors have obtained valuable suggestions on how to improve production for all enumerators.

While supervisors are instructed to examine quantity within the fixed framework of quality, it appears that in some cases the qualitative aspects may be overlooked. This arises from two causes. First, in many instances it is impossible, without rechecking the interviewer's work, to distinguish an accurately filled out questionnaire from an inaccurate but internally consistent questionnaire. The amount of rechecking that is carried through with the quality control program now in operation is quite limited. Second, production quotas and levels of performance are established by means of quantitative measures. With this situation there is a great tendency for supervisors, when having something objective and concrete, to be overinfluenced by this factor.

The current position of the Bureau of the Census with respect to interviewer production quotas is outlined in General Administrative Memorandum No. 253 (Supplement No. V), which follows.

DEPARTMENT OF COMMERCE
Bureau of the Census
Washington 25, D.C.

February 4, 1954

GENERAL ADMINISTRATIVE MEMORANDUM NO. 253 (Supplement No. V)

To: All Regional Supervisors
All District Supervisors

From: Jack B. Robertson
Chief, Field Division

Subject: Control of Enumeration in CPS and CCBR Programs

Contents

A. INTRODUCTION

Production guides applicable to enumerators working on current programs were first transmitted to the field in General Administrative Memorandum No. 253, October 16, 1953. After initial field experience with these standards, certain revisions in allowances have been transmitted as Supplement No. IV to the above memorandum.

The record of the Field Division in the continuing improvement of its standards of performance indicates that each of you has recognized your responsibility to accomplish quality work at a minimum cost. It is important, however, that we review at this time the supervisory tools we are using in order to assure the maintenance of our record.

This memorandum is intended to help toward that end. It discusses the purpose and content of the standards program; it suggests methods for supervisory analysis of individual enumerator performance and outlines methods for taking corrective action when indicated. Your suggestions for refinement of the methods discussed are invited.

B. ELEMENTS OF EFFECTIVE CONTROL

The objective of control is to accomplish work of acceptable quality, on time and at a minimum cost. To achieve effective control, we must establish standards of quality, progress and cost for the work, check actual performance against the standards, and take prompt action when performance varies too far from standard. Before reviewing these techniques in detail, there are certain general points to be made.

(more)

Control means action to keep costs and quality within the specifications. Effective control, therefore, requires correct reports submitted on time. Reports obtained too late for action are useful only as history, not for control. The timeliness required in reports will, of course, depend upon the kind of action to be taken. In operations which are characterized by relatively short periods of work occurring each month, such as CPS or CCBR, certain supervisory steps are intended to affect the current month's enumeration while others will be looking toward the following month. For example, the supervisor must know promptly each month whether all his enumerators are starting out on time and continuing to work. Failures on either score require immediate attention. On the other hand, excessive use of man hours or mileage by an enumerator would usually be dealt with during the following month's enumeration. Here the information must be available in time to analyze the problem and plan the corrective action to be taken: e.g., memorandum or telephone call, prior to the following month, or observation of the next enumeration.

When performance fails to meet standards, an investigation of the reason must be made and corrective action taken immediately. Prompt follow-up is especially important, since poor performance, when tolerated, tends to justify itself and to become the new standard. When that happens, our achieving the proper standard can be a difficult process, one engendering resentment between supervisor and employees.

In order for the supervisor to take remedial action, control procedures must provide a way of tracing excessive costs or poor quality to individual phases of his operations or to individual persons. This means that standards must be established, and reports obtained for each important phase of the operation and for each person involved.

Not only should there be standards established for each person, but every person should know the standard of performance expected of him. There is a common belief in this regard that the way to achieve the most efficient job is to set people to work without standards but to tell them that they must work as efficiently as possible. This belief, however, has been discredited by experience. The fallacy may be attractive in theory, but it develops in practice that most people work better when given some goal, such as a standard. Moreover, since the supervisor will, in any event, be forming opinions about his people, it is only fair that his employees know the standards against which they will be judged. A clearly understood standard also helps to forestall many of the problems of trying to catch up with--rather than to prevent--inadequate work.

Good reports and methods for measuring performance against standards are aids in supervision. They are neither a substitute for, nor are they in conflict with the supervisor's experiences and judgment. Rather, they provide facts on the basis of which the supervisor can plan his work. They relieve the supervisor of time-consuming detail, and leave him free to concentrate on evaluation and improvement.

(more)

C. SETTING STANDARDS

We have noted that experience indicates that enumerators should be given standards of performance from the start. Fortunately, this experience has also shown that a "reasonable" standard properly used will achieve almost as much as a "perfect" one.

It was only natural, then, to turn to CPS experience in the 68-area sample and CCBR experience in the new 230-area sample, to see what information might be available for setting preliminary standards as goals in the early months of CPS redesign. This was done, and initial standards were set.

The standards provide a means of measuring the "efficiency" of individual enumerators and of District Office field functions, ("efficiency" being defined as the standard allowance divided by actual cost). This efficiency measure has certain desirable properties. For fixed workload the standard allowance remains fixed. Therefore, in the case of cost, for example, as actual cost goes down the efficiency measure goes up, and vice versa. Further, a deviation of the efficiency measure from the value 1.00 (standard efficiency) can be considered as a percent deviation. For example, an efficiency score of .97 would mean an operation of 97% efficiency or 3% below standard. Similarly, and efficiency score of 1.10 would mean an operation at 110% efficiency or 10% above standard.

D. ACCEPTABLE LIMITS OF VARIATION IN EFFICIENCY

The acceptable limits of variation in efficiency for enumerators is .50 to 1.50 for each of CCBR hours, CPS hours, and for mileage. The acceptable limits for District Office field efficiency are shown, for each office, in the table attached to the memorandum. The District Office limits allow for less variation in efficiency than the limits for an individual enumerator, since differences between enumerators tend to average out at the District Office level. Moreover, because of this averaging effect, the larger the District Office workload, the smaller the variation in efficiency allowed.

The interpretation of the enumerator limits is as follows:

1. Performance of persons whose efficiency ratio is less than .50 or more than 1.50 in any one month should be investigated and action taken by the following month.

2. Performance of persons whose efficiency ratio is between .50 and .75 or between 1.25 and 1.50 should be watched. Investigation and follow-up action should then be taken for any person with this pattern of efficiency in 3 successive months. The District Office limits have a similar interpretation based on the values given in the table attached.

(more)

E. INTERPRETATION AND USE OF THE STANDARDS

The system of standards and allowable limits of variability in efficiency should be regarded as an objective tool for evaluating on a uniform basis the performance of individuals and of District Offices. The standards provide a measure against which to compare any individual, taking into account, of course, those characteristics of his assignment that might significantly affect performance. Comparing the individual against the standard for his particular assignment thus avoids the problems inherent in comparing individuals with each other when their assignments may be of varying difficulty.

The purpose of the limits of variation is to screen out those persons whose efficiency is so low, or so high, that the chances are that investigation and follow-up action will be profitable. This does not mean that individuals "within limits" could not show improvement. What it does mean is that we can be reasonably certain that less would be accomplished by the supervisor's concentrating on those "within limits" than on the groups "outside limits". Of course, a supervisor would concentrate upon the extreme cases, based on his judgment and experience. The advantage of the limits of variation for identifying the extremes is that they give the supervisor an objective screen which takes into account all of our experience, in other District Offices as well as his own; and, in addition, makes for uniformity among all offices in the criteria by which enumerators are to be judged.

F. TYPES OF INVESTIGATION AND FOLLOW-UP ACTION

When an individual is found with efficiency outside limits, the first point on which to check is whether the report of performance (hours and mileage) is correct. This is especially important in the case of persons showing efficiencies of 2.50 or more. If the report is found to be correct, priority for investigation should be given to enumerators with low efficiency.

Low efficiency will probably be due to one of two causes: (1) the person is not exerting much effort, or (2) the person is using inefficient procedures. Accordingly, the assignment should be carefully reviewed from these points of view. Particular ingenuity may be necessary in the case of enumerators. Here, prior to consulting with the enumerator, the supervisor should review the maps of the area assigned to the enumerator, the progress and callback problems as indicated by dates and calls recorded on the schedules, and the like. This review may disclose a problem which can be resolved by memorandum or telephone call to the enumerator. It may be, however, that the problem can only be identified or resolved by visit to the sample area to observe the enumerator at work.

(more)

It must be emphasized that the standards established for each area are based on average conditions. Therefore, if the enumerator encounters special problems such as unusual callback or travel requirements, his efficiency ratio will necessarily be low. It is the responsibility of the supervisor in such cases to (1) document the facts of the problem; and (2) attempt to devise methods of planning or carrying out the work so that the efficiency ratio will be raised to the level of other areas, or, if this is not possible, to submit the documentation to the Chief, Field Division, with a request for revision of the allowances.

Cases of high efficiency ratios may indicate, assuming correct reporting, an enumerator who is more than usually conscientious; or one who may have found short cuts in doing the work. Unusual conscientiousness should, of course, be promptly acknowledged and the enumerator commended. In the case of short cuts, a check should be made of the circumstances.

One type of short cut an enumerator may take is to lower the quality of his work--turning in a high non-interview rate, sloppy schedules that fail edit, and the like. The quality of work should be checked in the case of every enumerator, of course, but especially in the case of an enumerator with an unusually high efficiency ratio. Deficiencies of this kind must be brought to the enumerator's attention promptly.

If the enumerator is found to have actually developed an efficient work procedure, this should be acknowledged and the enumerator commended. Reports of such procedures should be forwarded to the Chief, Field Division, so that they may be reviewed for possible general circulation and for consideration under the employee suggestion award system. This review may also show, occasionally, that a suggested procedure can be expected to have a damaging effect on the quality of data obtained which was not immediately apparent, so that the procedure must be abandoned.

This discussion is merely illustrative in nature and supervisors can expect to encounter a wide variety of situations. In every case, however, the supervisor should carefully prepare his facts in advance before proceeding with the individual concerned.

G. REVISION OF STANDARDS

As work progresses in the new sample, the standards and allowable limits of variation established will be revised on the basis of experience. Within the next few months, we hope to initiate a program of time-studies of field operations, which will also serve as the basis for revising standards. As the standards are improved, it will be possible to tighten up the allowable limits of variation, by eliminating the extra margin now included to take account of approximations in the present standards.

(more)

In general, the supervisor should start with the assumption that the current standard established is the appropriate one. Reports concerning areas or operations for which the allowances appear to be too high should be sent to the Chief, Field Division, with the Supervisor's recommendations as to appropriate allowances. As noted in paragraph F above, reports concerning areas for which the allowances appear to be too low should similarly be sent to the Chief, Field Division, with adequate documentation.

H. PROBLEMS IN SUPERVISOR PLANNING

There are two ways in which the supervisor will be working to improve performance: (1) raising the average level of performance, and (2) reducing the variation in efficiency from person to person.

Because of the fact that we are initially starting with large numbers of new personnel, supervisors can expect that perhaps a fourth to a third of their enumerators will differ from standard by more than the allowable limits of variation (that is, below .50 or above 1.50). With proper follow-up and adjustment of allowances these differences should level off rapidly. Considering the problems of recruitment and training and of turnover in personnel, it is urgent that each supervisor keep on top of his job by adequate planning. This means that:

1. The supervisor's reports and analyses must be kept up to date.

2. Immediately upon completion of each month's CPS or CCBR work the supervisor must know what problems he will face during the <u>next</u> month, including allowance for problems of expected turnover, leave, etc.

3. If the supervisor will not be able to deal with the problems he forsees, in the time available to him and his staff, he must promptly request additional assistance from his Regional Supervisor. We have available to us, in addition to Regional Staff, staff from the Bureau in Washington. It is expected that these resources will be adequate for the needs that may arise.

Attachment

Attachment
GEN. ADMIN. MEMO. NO. 253 (Supp. V)
February 4, 1954

ALLOWABLE LIMITS OF VARIATION IN DISTRICT OFFICE EFFICIENCY FOR FIELD WORK

Note: Efficiencies beyond those in this table should be investigated for causes (Figures apply separately to each of CCBR hours, CPS hours, and mileage. Equivalent limits for individual enumerators are .50 - 1.50)

District-Office		Limits
No.	Name	
141	Boston, Massachusetts	.85 - 1.15
161	Hartford, Connecticut	.80 - 1.20
211	New York, New York	.90 - 1.10
212	Rochester, New York	.75 - 1.25
231	Philadelphia, Pennsylvania	.85 - 1.15
232	Pittsburgh, Pennsylvania	.80 - 1.20
311	Cleveland, Ohio	.80 - 1.20
312	Hamilton, Ohio	.80 - 1.20
321	Indianapolis, Indiana	.80 - 1.20
331	Chicago, Illinois	.85 - 1.15
341	Detroit, Michigan	.85 - 1.15
351	Milwaukee, Wisconsin	.80 - 1.20
411	St. Paul, Minnesota	.80 - 1.20
421	Des Moines, Iowa	.80 - 1.20
431	St. Louis, Missouri	.80 - 1.20
432	Kansas City, Missouri	.80 - 1.20
521	Baltimore, Maryland	.80 - 1.20
541	Norfolk, Virginia	.75 - 1.25
561	Charlotte, North Carolina	.80 - 1.20
581	Atlanta, Georgia	.80 - 1.20
591	Sarasota, Florida	.75 - 1.25
621	Johnson City, Tennessee	.60 - 1.40
631	Birmingham, Alabama	.75 - 1.25
641	Gulfport, Mississippi	.70 - 1.30
642	Clarksdale, Mississippi	.70 - 1.30
711	Hot Springs, Arkansas	.70 - 1.30
741	Houston, Texas	.80 - 1.20
742	Dallas, Texas	.80 - 1.20
841	Boulder, Colorado	.65 - 1.35
851	Roswell, New Mexico	.70 - 1.30
871	Salt Lake City, Utah	.55 - 1.45
911	Seattle, Washington	.80 - 1.20
931	Los Angeles, California	.85 - 1.15
932	San Francisco, California	.80 - 1.20

APPENDIX 10

A Partial Test of the Samples Based on the 1940 and 1950 Population Censuses

A partial test can be made of the representativeness of the 68 areas that were selected for the old survey and the 230 areas that are used in the new survey by means of data that were obtained for these and all other areas of the continental United States in the decennial population censuses. This test is applied only to the first step in the selection of the sample since it does not include the further step of drawing a sample of dwelling units within each of the selected areas. In other words, it shows how representative the selected areas would have been if all the households in each of the areas had been interviewed in the survey and then estimates for the entire population of the United States had been prepared from the data for the areas. To make the comparison completely valid, the method of preparing these estimates should be the same as that used in the monthly surveys, except that it is not based on a sample of households within the areas. In addition, military personnel and persons who live in institutions should be excluded. The data for counties are not available in sufficient detail to allow an estimation procedure in these comparisons identical with the ratio estimate procedure used in the monthly surveys, but a procedure as similar as possible has been used.

The results of such an estimating process and comparable figures from the full census enumeration are given in Table 1. The principal differences that are revealed in the 68-area comparison are an excess of farmers, a deficiency of employed men other than farmers, and an excess of employed women. In the 230-area comparison there is also a deficiency of employed men other than farmers. Both sets of areas appear to be quite representative of the number of persons who were unemployed in April 1950 as they were reported in the population census. In this comparison it should be noted that the April 1950 Current Population Survey produced an estimate of the number of persons who were unemployed that was more than 600,000 greater than that of the comparable count in the population census. A check of 51,000 persons as they were actually reported in both the survey and the census showed that almost all this difference was due to interviewing and response rather than sampling. Because of this substantial difference between the census and survey processes, there may be some discrepancies that the comparison would reveal if it were based on data obtained by the survey interviewers. Another limitation of the comparison is the fact that the data were obtained in the spring, i.e. in April, and at a particular level of unemployment,

Table 1.--LABOR FORCE STATISTICS FROM COMPLETE CENSUS COMPARED WITH ESTIMATES* FROM 230-AREA AND 68-AREA COUNTY SAMPLES BASED ON COMPLETE CENSUS TOTALS FOR THE SAMPLE COUNTIES: APRIL 1950

(In thousands)

Characteristic	1950 complete census	230-area sample	68-area sample	Difference between 1950 census and 230-area sample	Difference between 1950 census and 68-area sample	Difference between 230-area and 68-area samples	Estimated standard error of difference (B-C)
	A	B	C	A-B	A-C	B-C	
Total Population 14 Years Old and Over							
Total labor force..........	59,070	58,870	59,190	200	-120	-320	400
Employed................	56,240	56,030	56,340	210	-100	-310	**
Farmers and farm mgrs..	4,310	4,290	4,420	20	-110	-130	**
Unemployed..............	2,830	2,840	2,850	-10	-20	-10	100
Not in labor force.........	52,300	52,500	52,180	-200	120	320	400
Male							
Total labor force..........	42,600	42,390	42,480	210	120	-90	**
Employed................	40,520	40,300	40,390	220	130	-90	**
Farmers and farm mgrs..	4,190	4,180	4,270	10	-80	-90	**
Unemployed..............	2,080	2,090	2,090	-10	-10	0	**
Not in labor force.........	11,760	11,970	11,880	-210	-120	90	**
Female							
Total labor force..........	16,470	16,480	16,710	-10	-240	-230	**
Employed................	15,720	15,730	15,950	-10	-230	-220	**
Farmers and farm mgrs..	116	114	151	2	-35	-37	**
Unemployed..............	750	750	760	0	-10	-10	**
Not in labor force.........	40,540	40,530	40,300	10	240	230	**

* Involve approximations to the race-residence and age-sex-race ratio estimates used in the CPS (based on 1950 Census data). The complete census data are not available in sufficient detail to make identical ratio estimates possible. **Not computed.

whereas the difference between the 68-area estimates and the 230-area estimates that led to the present inquiry was observed in January and under somewhat different conditions in the labor market. Within these limitations, it may be concluded that the set of 230 areas that were selected and also the set of 68 areas that had been used for the old survey were reasonably representative when taken as the basis for the labor force sample estimates of the civilian noninstitutional population of the United States. Even in this comparison, however, there is some evidence of the inevitable variation that is introduced by the selection of a sample. Under the design of the 230-area survey, the greater part of the sampling variation that is to be expected will occur in the second stage of sampling; namely, that of selecting the small groups of dwelling units or "segments" within each of the 230 areas. This is not tested, unfortunately, by the comparisons shown in Table 1.

A further comparison for the 230 areas was prepared by the staff of the Census Bureau at the request of the Committee (see Table 2). For most of the items it goes beyond the degree of subdivision that is likely to be made in the labor force estimates in the near future but it shows a reassuring similarity between the estimates for several industry, occupation, and income groups that were selected to reveal any gross lack of representativeness that might exist between the 230 areas and the population they represent.

A similar comparison was made for the Committee to show the representativeness of the 230 areas for a division of the United States into four major regions (see Table 3). It shows a similar degree of representativeness but in several instances there is a greater difference than is likely to be acceptable, considering that in addition to the difference shown there would be a further variation due to sampling within the areas. This leaves a question as to whether the 230-area sample survey will be suitable for such regional estimates for more than a few of the most stable items.

Since the 230 areas were selected with the aid of the data covering the period 1940-1950, and in particular using industry data by counties for 1948 and preliminary population counts from the 1950 census,* one might question whether they will become less representative as time passes. It is true that the benefit derived

---

*Only this item from the 1950 Census was available at the time the sample was drawn.

Table 2.--ILLUSTRATIVE DATA--COMPLETE CENSUS STATISTICS COMPARED WITH ESTIMATES* FROM 230-AREA COUNTY SAMPLE BASED ON COMPLETE CENSUS TOTALS FOR THE SAMPLE COUNTIES, BY SEX: APRIL 1950

(In thousands)

Item	Total			Male			Female		
	1950 complete census	230-area sample		1950 complete census	230-area sample		1950 complete census	230-area sample	
		Number	Percent of 1950 census		Number	Percent of 1950 census		Number	Percent of 1950 census
	Number of Employed Persons								
Specified major industry groups:									
Construction..........	3,440	3,449	100.3	3,342	3,352	100.3	98	97	99.0
Elec. mach., equipment and supplies.........	789	747	94.7	514	490	95.3	275	256	93.1
Motor vehicles and motor vehicle equip..	869	866	99.7	759	759	100.0	109	106	97.2
Textile mill products.	1,240	1,157	93.3	713	672	94.2	528	485	91.9
Apparel and other fabricated textile products.............	1,063	1,055	99.2	311	309	99.4	753	746	99.1
Railroads and railway express service......	1,386	1,391	100.4	1,313	1,314	100.1	73	76	104.1
Specified major occupational groups:									
Sales workers.........	3,927	3,871	98.6	2,597	2,544	98.0	1,330	1,327	99.8
Operatives and kindred workers.............	11,140	10,919	98.0	8,120	7,971	98.2	3,020	2,948	97.6
	Number of Families and Unrelated Individuals								
Income in 1949:									
Less than $500........	6,210	6,310	101.6	xxx	xxx	xxx	xxx	xxx	xxx
$2,500 to $2,999......	4,056	4,051	99.9	xxx	xxx	xxx	xxx	xxx	xxx
$7,000 to $9,999......	1,841	1,831	99.5	xxx	xxx	xxx	xxx	xxx	xxx

* Include ratio estimates for number of persons 14 years and over by sex, as an approximation to the age-sex-race ratio estimates used in CPS (based on 1950 Census data). The complete census data are not available in sufficient detail to make the race-residence and more detailed age-sex-race ratio estimates possible.

Table 3.--ILLUSTRATIVE DATA--COMPLETE CENSUS STATISTICS COMPARED WITH ESTIMATES* FROM 230-AREA COUNTY SAMPLE BASED ON COMPLETE CENSUS TOTALS FOR THE SAMPLE COUNTIES, BY REGIONS: APRIL 1950

(In thousands)

Item	Northeast			North Central		
	1950 complete census	230-area sample		1950 complete census	230-area sample	
		Number	Percent of 1950 census		Number	Percent of 1950 census
	Number of Employed Persons					
Specified major industry groups:						
Construction..............	851	849	99.8	907	863	95.1
Elec. mach. equipment and supplies...........	392	409	104.3	331	280	84.6
Motor vehicles and motor vehicle equip....	98	92	93.9	708	715	101.0
Textile mill products...	554	486	87.7	56	64	114.3
Apparel and other fabricated textile products.	667	677	101.5	161	154	95.7
Railroads and railway express service........	333	358	107.5	499	468	93.8
Specified major occupation groups:						
Sales workers............	1,106	1,109	100.3	1,205	1,174	97.4
Operatives and kindred workers...............	3,719	3,647	98.1	3,419	3,363	98.4
	Number of Families and Unrelated Individuals					
Income in 1949:						
Less than $500..........	1,461	1,467	100.4	1,656	1,685	101.8
$2,500 to $2,999.........	1,193	1,186	99.4	1,272	1,263	99.3
$7,000 to $9,999........	588	583	99.1	598	588	98.3

Table 3.--ILLUSTRATIVE DATA--COMPLETE CENSUS STATISTICS COMPARED WITH ESTIMATES* FROM 230-AREA COUNTY SAMPLE BASED ON COMPLETE CENSUS TOTALS FOR THE SAMPLE COUNTIES, BY REGIONS: APRIL 1950--Con.

(In thousands)

Item	South			West		
	1950 complete census	230-area sample		1950 complete census	230-area sample	
		Number	Percent of 1950 census		Number	Percent of 1950 census
	Number of Employed Persons					
Specified major industry groups:						
Construction............	1,128	1,120	99.3	554	618	111.6
Elec. mach. equipment and supplies...........	36	29	80.6	29	28	96.6
Motor vehicles and motor vehicle equip....	35	30	85.7	28	28	100.0
Textile mill products...	617	595	96.4	15	13	86.7
Apparel and other fabricated textile products.	180	169	93.9	57	55	96.5
Railroads and railway express service........	368	374	101.6	186	191	102.7
Specified major occupation groups:						
Sales workers...........	1,053	1,050	99.7	562	538	95.7
Operatives and kindred workers...............	2,952	2,925	99.1	1,050	983	93.6
	Number of Families and Unrelated Individuals					
Income in 1949:						
Less than $500.........	2,386	2,436	102.1	707	684	96.7
$2,500 to $2,999........	1,043	1,040	99.7	548	536	97.8
$7,000 to $9,999........	357	349	97.8	298	300	100.7

* Include ratio estimates for number of persons 14 years and over by sex, as an approximation to the age-sex-race ratio estimate used in CPS (based on 1950 Census data). The complete census data are not available in sufficient detail to make the race-residence and more detailed age-sex-race ratio estimates possible.

from the use of these data for stratification in the selection of the areas will diminish as various changes occur in the population with the passing of time. The loss may not be very great, however, and the selected areas will still be a proper sample of all the areas that might have been selected, providing the remainder of the sampling operation necessary to obtain samples of households in each area is performed correctly. The representativeness of the 230 areas was also tested with the data for the 1940 census (see Table 4). The 230-area sample turned out to be even more closely representative of the population in 1940 than in 1950 and closer than the 68 areas in 1940. This is significant in assessing the relative accuracy of the old and new surveys since the 68 areas were selected with the use of data from the 1940 census and, therefore, might have been expected to turn out better in this comparison.

These comparisons are only a partial test of the samples. They do not test the sampling of households within areas, the lack of information about households that could not be interviewed successfully, or the changes from the time of the census to the time of the survey and from one set of labor force categories to another. None the less, they do provide a check on one of the principal differences between the old sample and the new one that leads us to believe that the selection of the 230 areas for the present labor force survey is not one of the sources that may have produced major differences between the two surveys.

Table 4.--LABOR FORCE STATISTICS FROM COMPLETE CENSUS COMPARED WITH ESTIMATES* FROM 230-AREA AND 68-AREA COUNTY SAMPLES BASED ON COMPLETE CENSUS TOTALS FOR THE SAMPLE COUNTIES: APRIL 1940

(In thousands)

Characteristic	1940 complete census	230-area sample	68-area sample	Difference between 1940 census and 230-area sample	Difference between 1940 census and 68-area sample	Difference between 230-area and 68-area samples
	A	B	C	A-B	A-C	B-C
Total Population 14 Years old and Over						
Total labor force	52,789	52,848	52,597	-59	192	251
Employed	45,166	45,176	45,061	-10	105	115
Farmers and farm managers	5,144	5,191	5,101	-47	43	90
Unemployed	7,623	7,672	7,536	-49	87	136
Not in labor force	48,314	48,255	48,506	59	-192	-251
Male						
Total labor force	39,944	39,887	39,749	57	195	138
Employed	34,028	33,950	33,887	78	141	63
Farmers and farm managers	4,992	5,003	4,930	-11	62	73
Unemployed	5,916	5,937	5,862	-21	54	75
Not in labor force	10,610	10,667	10,805	-57	-195	-138
Female						
Total labor force	12,845	12,961	12,848	-116	-3	113
Employed	11,138	11,226	11,174	-88	-36	52
Farmers and farm managers	152	187	171	-35	-19	16
Unemployed	1,707	1,735	1,674	-28	33	61
Not in labor force	37,704	37,588	37,701	116	3	-113

* Involve approximations to the race-residence and age-sex-race ratio estimates used in the CPS (based on 1940 Census data). The complete census data are not available in sufficient detail to make identical ratio estimates possible.

APPENDIX 11

The Accuracy of the Estimates in the Current Population Survey

The usefulness of the information that is supplied by surveys like the Current Population Survey, which provides the data for the Monthly Report on the Labor Force, is greatly limited if the user of the information does not have a trustworthy and fairly definite indication of its accuracy. Unfortunately this is one of the most difficult kinds of appraisal since there is usually no more accurate source of information against which to test the estimates. One is forced to resort to a technical analysis of the processes by which the data are produced and to use various indirect tests, some of which raise more questions than they answer.

The Census Bureau has been one of the pioneers in the analysis and testing of accuracy of sample surveys. Thus it has published with the monthly report, though not in the press releases, its estimates of the degree of uncertainty in the labor force figures that is a result of sampling variation and variation in response. The other sources of inaccuracy and uncertainty are mentioned, however, only in general terms without any estimate of their magnitude. The reader must do what he can to supply them or else make a general reservation to allow for their influence in his use of the labor force estimates. Unfortunately his problem is eased very little by the fact that he is in the same predicament in other fields of statistics.

One of the indirect tests of accuracy is that provided by such comparisons as could be made between the 68-area and 230-area surveys during the period in which they were both in operation. The discrepancy in the estimates of unemployment is a timely warning that there are sources of inaccuracy that exceed those shown by the usual tables of sampling error. It is important to be alerted for such extreme divergence. It is also important to avoid excessive skepticism since one may then get no use at all from figures that do have real value if they are used with discretion. The discrepancy in the estimates of unemployment is paralleled by differences in the estimates of persons who had a job but were not working in the survey week and of those who worked from 1 to 14 hours, 15 to 34 hours, or 35 and more hours in that week. In contrast to these major differences, the old and new survey estimates in January 1954 agreed within 1 percent in the case of such categories as private wage or salary employment, government employment, employment in manufacturing, employment in service industries, and average hours worked in the survey week. Estimates of many other categories were within

5 percent of agreement. This is evidence pointing to the inadvisability of discarding all the recent results of the old survey since many of them may be about as accurate as the results currently provided by the 230-area survey. What is needed is more information about the accuracy of each major item so that it may be used to the full extent of its usefulness but no further.

The Committee gave some attention to the estimation of sampling errors. In the past these have been computed by the Census Bureau for only some of the characteristics of the labor force and at relatively infrequent dates. They have been recomputed at about 2-year intervals but for most months all the estimates of accuracy were taken from computations made some time earlier by means of a relationship that appeared to hold between the size of the estimate and its estimated sampling variation. For some items this was done even in the month in which the estimates of variation were recomputed. This was done to increase the accuracy of the estimated sampling errors, since with the 68-area sample such estimates necessarily were made from a relatively few independent observations. It was also used to supply estimated sampling errors for many detailed items without excessive computing and was almost unavoidable in the face of the complexity of the job of supplying a separately computed estimate for each of the many items in the report on the labor force. The present use of electronic computing equipment for the preparation of labor force estimates should permit a more extensive and more frequent computation of their sampling errors. Inasmuch as the Census Bureau is preparing an extensive report on this subject, there is no need of a full discussion here of the methods of estimating the sampling errors of the estimates.

The Census Bureau has reported its provisional estimate that the sampling error of estimates of unemployment will exceed 4 percent about one third of the time and 8 percent about one time in twenty. This looks uncomfortably large, especially since it might increase substantially when changes in the labor market make it more difficult to ascertain unemployment. There is not enough safety margin for unforeseen contingencies. Moreover, even this degree of accuracy cannot be maintained when the sample is further subdivided into finer classifications and smaller categories to meet urgent needs for new information. This is the principal basis for the Committee's recommendation that the sample be enlarged.

Concurrently with an enlargement of the sample it is important to eliminate as much as possible of the inaccuracy that results from incomplete coverage of the sample and error in the interviews. To some extent this can be done by better use of the methods now available to select and train interviewers and to conduct the field work. A considerable part of it can be done only after some exacting research studies have brought to light the causes of inaccuracy and developed effective methods of controlling or eliminating them. The first problems to be tackled in these studies should be the effect of taking repeated interviews from the same households and the sources of inaccuracy that may be peculiar to the first interview. This will probably require the use of a sample design somewhat different from that of the 230-area survey but one that is tied in with it as a moderate supplementary sample. It will also require a small staff of specially trained interviewers (who have broad knowledge of labor force survey problems and are drawn from higher echelons of the Census Bureau staff) and some variation in the usual field procedures.

The estimation of systematic inaccuracy beyond that which is included in the present estimates of sampling error will require extensive checking of survey data against information in other record systems and even by actual observation. The latter may be necessary to discover some of the sources of error in interviewing, and one of the first places it can be done is in the district offices and other places from which telephone interviews are conducted.

The use of recheck interviews should be increased and additional efforts should be made to discover the reasons for inconsistency between some of the original interview results and the results of the recheck interviews for the same persons.

More attention should be given to the households that are not interviewed because of temporary absence, illness, and similar reasons. Each month such noninterviews amount to from 3 to 5 percent of the sample. The households not interviewed may be a negligible proportion of the population in many of the labor force categories but they may also be a substantially greater proportion of some of the lesser categories such as "with a job but not at work." The possibility of obtaining information for such households for research and improvement of the estimates, even though it cannot be obtained in time to be included in the regular tabulations, should be exploited. This is especially true in the system of recheck interviews since they may overstate the reliability of interviewing and fail to discover some of the systematic error if they succeed in completing only 85 to 90 percent of the interviews selected for recheck.

The testing and improvement of accuracy are connected in many ways with the problems of revising the concepts and classifications that are used in labor force surveys. Greater accuracy can be obtained by a suitable revision of the categories, especially in the direction of simplicity and compression, but this may reduce the usefulness of the information. Likewise the accuracy may be reduced greatly if a more difficult set of categories is adopted. For these reasons the conceptual problems and the problems of accuracy should be considered in conjunction. The value of the survey results depends on a sound assignment of the weight to be given to each of the problems that affect them. Greater resources in personnel and budget are needed for the improvement of operations and for operating studies as well as for the enlargement of the survey and strengthening of the controls. More attention should be given, too, to the explanation of the results to the users and to the discovery and correction of their misunderstandings, since the accuracy that counts is that which users achieve in their understanding and use of the survey information.

APPENDIX 12

The New Composite Estimating Procedure

The estimates of the labor force are prepared from the recorded interviews by a procedure that involves a number of steps and makes use of population estimates that are independent of the survey. A description of the procedure is given in Appendix 5, page A-27 f. There is one aspect of the procedure, however, that was investigated in some detail by the Committee, namely the new "composite estimate" that is formed as the last step in the process. The composite estimate was introduced in the 230-area survey for February and has been used each month since then. It combines the results of the current month with the final estimate of the preceding month after the latter has been brought up to date by an estimate of the change that occurred during the intervening period. This estimate of change is obtained from the households in segments that were in the survey in both months. Thus half of the estimate is the regular ratio estimate computed from the current month's interviews and half is the composite estimate for the previous month plus the estimated change based on the households in segments common to the two months. For example, the estimate of the number of unemployed persons in June 1954 is completed by the following step:

	Thousands
The composite estimate for May 1954 was	3,305
The change from May to June in the part of the sample that was in both the May survey and the June survey, when expanded to be an estimate for the whole population was	3
The May estimate brought up to June, then, was .	3,308
The regular ratio estimate for June from the sample that was in the June survey was	3,385
The composite estimate for June formed by taking an average of 3,308 and 3,385 was	3,347

Ordinarily, the change from month to month is greater than shown in this example.

The objective of the composite method is to increase the accuracy of the survey estimates of level of employment, unemployment, and other aspects of the labor force during any one survey week, of month-to-month changes, and of changes over longer periods of time. If it were not for the rotation of the sample, there would be no difference between the estimates for the first purpose and those for the second. The composite method would give the same results as the method that was used previously. The effect of rotation is to divide the sample covered in any month into two parts, one common to the current and preceding month and the other included in the current month but not the preceding month. Often, a more accurate estimate of change than is obtained as the difference between the regular ratio estimates for two succeeding months can be computed by giving greater weight to the part that is common to the two months than to the parts that are not common. The composite method is one way of doing just this. Such an estimate will be more accurate provided the correlation between estimates made from identical segments is sufficiently high. There are, however, certain possible types of bias or distortion in the survey process that could prevent the achievement of this greater accuracy.

The composite estimates were computed for employment and unemployment in each month of the six years, 1948 to 1953, as a test of the performance of the method. The results are given in Table 1. Most of the estimates differed by negligible amounts from the figures that had been published but there were several months in which the two sets of figures differed by more than 100,000 for nonagricultural employment and by more than 50,000 for agricultural employment. In the case of unemployment there were similar differences but, while some of the composite estimates of employment were higher than the original estimates, most of the composite estimates of unemployment were lower than the original figures. On the average, they were more than 50,000 lower. While its behavior during this period may not be completely representative of the performance of the composite estimating method in the future, it suggests pretty strongly the existence of a persistent difference in unemployment estimates by the two methods. Research into the causes of this difference is needed before final acceptance of the new estimation procedure can be justified.

The composite method has not been used long enough in the new 230-area survey to permit an assessment of its accuracy or its tendency toward over or underestimation. The data available for this period are given in Table 2. In each of the first six months it has shown a lower estimate than the regular ratio estimate. However, the apparent difference may not persist since it has diminished during the period. Also, since each estimate includes half the preceding month's estimate, the differences are likely to be similar in succeeding months, i.e., they are likely to occur in runs of the same sign and similar size. The consequence of this is

Table 1.--REGULAR RATIO ESTIMATE AND COMPOSITE ESTIMATE OF NONAGRICULTURAL EMPLOYMENT, AGRICULTURAL EMPLOYMENT AND UNEMPLOYMENT AS A PERCENT OF THE POPULATION 14 YEARS OLD AND OVER, JANUARY 1948-DECEMBER 1953

Year and month		Nonagricultural employment		Agricultural employment		Unemployment	
		Regular ratio estimate[1]	Composite estimate	Regular ratio estimate[1]	Composite estimate	Regular ratio estimate[1]	Composite estimate
1948:	Jan......	46.94	[2]46.94	6.62	[2]6.62	1.90	[2]1.90
	Feb......	47.14	47.14	6.36	6.39	2.48	2.44
	Mar......	47.26	47.25	6.42	6.56	2.26	2.20
	Apr......	47.56	47.50	6.94	7.05	2.06	2.03
	May[3]....	47.50	47.45	7.30	7.32	1.60	1.56
	June[3]...	48.50	48.48	8.80	8.81	2.00	1.98
	July....	48.88	48.83	8.56	8.64	2.04	1.96
	Aug......	49.14	49.28	7.90	7.87	1.82	1.74
	Sept....	48.04	48.16	8.08	8.08	1.72	1.68
	Oct......	47.96	48.01	8.00	7.89	1.50	1.44
	Nov......	48.34	48.32	7.44	7.36	1.72	1.68
	Dec.[3]...	48.40	48.41	6.90	6.88	1.80	1.79
1949:	Jan......	47.04	47.12	6.32	6.35	2.48	2.44
	Feb......	46.62	46.62	6.48	6.62	2.98	2.91
	Mar......	46.66	46.59	6.86	6.84	2.96	2.94
	Apr......	46.36	46.52	7.26	7.30	2.76	2.65
	May......	46.04	46.18	8.28	8.34	3.06	2.90
	June[3]...	46.20	46.29	9.00	9.02	3.50	3.45
	July....	46.30	46.34	8.90	8.91	3.80	3.78
	Aug......	47.50	47.52	7.90	7.90	3.40	3.39
	Sept....	47.32	47.27	7.52	7.76	3.06	3.02
	Oct......	47.26	47.16	7.12	7.25	3.26	3.14
	Nov......	47.54	47.50	7.28	7.36	3.16	3.05
	Dec.[3]...	47.60	47.60	6.20	6.23	3.20	3.18
1950:	Jan......	46.62	46.66	5.70	5.76	4.14	4.06
	Feb......	46.56	46.66	5.72	5.79	4.32	4.29
	Mar......	46.64	46.80	6.10	6.10	3.78	3.78
	Apr.[3]...	47.10	47.20	6.60	6.60	3.20	3.19
	May[3]....	47.30	47.35	7.40	7.40	2.80	2.80
	June....	47.90	47.98	8.28	8.34	3.08	2.94
	July....	48.20	48.19	7.72	7.78	2.92	2.83
	Aug......	49.46	49.42	7.42	7.45	2.24	2.18
	Sept....	48.74	48.83	7.10	7.02	2.12	2.15
	Oct......	48.68	48.60	7.80	7.76	1.78	1.76
	Nov......	49.18	48.94	6.90	6.98	2.06	2.01
	Dec.[3]...	49.60	49.47	5.70	5.74	2.00	2.00

[1] Based on weighted average of common and not-common rotation groups to provide estimate approximately equivalent to regular ratio estimate.

Table 1.--REGULAR RATIO ESTIMATE AND COMPOSITE ESTIMATE OF NONAGRICULTURAL EMPLOYMENT, AGRICULTURAL EMPLOYMENT AND UNEMPLOYMENT AS A PERCENT OF THE POPULATION 14 YEARS OLD AND OVER, JANUARY 1948-DECEMBER 1953--Con.

Year and month	Nonagricultural employment		Agricultural employment		Unemployment	
	Regular ratio estimate[1]	Composite estimate	Regular ratio estimate[1]	Composite estimate	Regular ratio estimate[1]	Composite estimate
1951: Jan......	48.54	48.60	5.48	5.46	2.30	2.20
Feb......	48.64	48.67	5.42	5.39	2.22	2.16
Mar......	49.32	49.24	5.90	5.94	1.96	1.86
Apr......	49.02	48.98	6.12	6.18	1.62	1.54
May......	49.40	49.34	6.86	6.92	1.48	1.46
June[3]....	49.40	49.37	7.40	7.46	1.80	1.78
July.....	50.16	49.96	7.28	7.32	1.72	1.70
Aug......	50.46	50.36	7.08	7.05	1.48	1.44
Sept.....	49.64	49.55	6.90	6.82	1.52	1.48
Oct......	49.68	49.72	7.06	6.94	1.52	1.50
Nov......	49.82	49.82	6.46	6.30	1.64	1.62
Dec.[3]....	50.00	50.01	5.80	5.75	1.50	1.46
1952: Jan......	49.02	49.16	5.64	5.60	1.88	1.77
Feb......	49.18	49.02	5.54	5.67	1.94	1.80
Mar......	49.16	49.04	5.54	5.66	1.66	1.58
Apr......	49.48	49.31	5.52	5.59	1.50	1.44
May......	49.52	49.36	6.40	6.60	1.44	1.44
June[3]....	49.70	49.63	7.50	7.60	1.70	1.67
July[3]....	49.80	49.76	6.90	6.95	1.80	1.78
Aug......	50.40	50.38	6.30	6.32	1.50	1.49
Sept.....	49.80	49.54	6.88	6.95	1.35	1.37
Oct......	49.62	49.48	6.58	6.56	1.12	1.10
Nov......	50.35	49.92	6.12	6.14	1.30	1.25
Dec......	50.48	50.10	5.18	5.21	1.22	1.14
1953: Jan......	49.75	49.48	5.05	5.08	1.68	1.51
Feb......	50.08	49.83	4.82	4.85	1.62	1.46
Mar......	50.10	50.06	5.18	5.16	1.52	1.34
Apr......	49.58	49.62	5.42	5.39	1.40	1.32
May......	49.62	49.67	5.75	5.57	1.18	1.10
June.....	49.52	49.54	7.10	6.98	1.40	1.35
July.....	49.80	49.72	6.85	6.76	1.42	1.38
Aug......	50.30	50.11	6.50	6.48	1.10	1.09
Sept.....	49.15	49.18	6.48	6.63	1.08	1.04
Oct......	49.20	49.24	6.35	6.49	.98	.91
Nov......	49.32	49.18	5.90	6.04	1.30	1.20
Dec......	49.28	49.03	4.78	4.96	1.62	1.56

[2] Initial composite estimate taken as January 1948 regular ratio estimate.
[3] No rotation of sample segments from preceding month.

Table 2.--COMPARISON OF REGULAR RATIO AND COMPOSITE ESTIMATES OF THE NUMBER OF PERSONS UNEMPLOYED, FEBRUARY TO JULY, 1954
(In thousands)

Month	Regular ratio estimate	Composite estimate	Difference
February..............	3,780	3,671	109
March.................	3,796	3,725	71
April.................	3,506	3,465	41
May...................	3,385	3,305	80
June..................	3,385	3,347	38
July..................	3,425	3,346	79

that a few months' data are not sufficient to exhibit the long-run behavior of the method. Until enough data have been accumulated and methods found to correct whatever bias there is in the use of the method, the application of the composite estimation procedure to the estimation of unemployment should be treated as experimental.

There is nothing in the composite estimation procedure as a method that necessarily leads to over or underestimation. The source of the difference observed is in the data to which the method is applied and it appears to be something that produces a higher rate of reported unemployment in households that are being interviewed for the first time than in households that have been interviewed before. There is no evidence yet to tell whether this is a matter of reporting too many unemployed persons in the first set of households or too few in the other households. It may be both. This uncertainty stands in the way of making an immediate correction based on the observed differences in previous months. A thoroughgoing research investigation of this problem is imperative. It must untangle (a) the differences due to real changes from month to month, (b) the differences due to change in the sample by removing and adding rotation groups of households, (c) the effect of the initial interview, and (d) the effect of the previous interviews on the information obtained from households that have been interviewed once, twice, or three times before. The difficulty of doing this untangling may be seen in Table 3.

Table 3.--ESTIMATES OF UNEMPLOYMENT FOR EACH ROTATION GROUP, MARCH TO JUNE, 1954

(In thousands)

Rotation group	March	April	May	June
A.......	950			
B.......	993	875		
C.......	964	912	897	
D.......	889	834	741	824
E.......		885	812	839
F.......			934	826
G.......				896
Total.........	3,796	3,506	3,384	3,385

If it were possible to measure the effect of the number of interviews that had been made previously with the households in a rotation group, the unemployment estimates could be corrected for the average biases found to be present. In the regular ratio estimates, such as those that were made from the 68-area sample, there is present the same effect of previous interviewing, but it is simply an average of the biases of zero, one, two and three immediately preceding interviews. In the composite estimates the start of the series may be similar to the regular ratio estimates in its inclusion of these effects, but as the series continues from month to month it settles down to a system in which the bias for households newly introduced into the sample is present with a weight of -1/12 and the bias for the households that have been in the sample for three preceding months, and are therefore scheduled to drop out of the sample in the succeeding month, will have a weight of +7/12 in the estimate for the current month. In the regular ratio estimates, the weight on each of these bias contributions is $+\frac{1}{4}$. If the first interview with a household is the most accurate and later interviews are biased in one direction, the composite estimates will have a greater bias than the regular ratio estimates, but if the first interviews have the greater bias and all biases are in the same direction, the regular ratio estimates will show the greater bias. The absence of information about the magnitude and direction of the biases connected with previous interviewing creates an unanswered question about the usefulness of the composite method and other possible methods of estimation. It is easy to show that some other sources of inaccuracy are reduced by the use of the composite method.

It should be noted that at the present time the magnitude of the difference between the regular ratio estimate and the composite is less than the standard error of either estimate, but if the sample size were increased considerably, it would become a more important factor in estimates of level.

There is as yet no important evidence that there is any upward or downward tendency in the composite estimates of employment. Data for the new survey are given in Table 4. Further tests

Table 4.--ESTIMATES OF AGRICULTURAL AND NONAGRICULTURAL EMPLOYMENT FOR EACH ROTATION GROUP, MARCH TO JUNE, 1954

(In thousands)

Rotation group	Agricultural employment				Nonagricultural employment			
	March	April	May	June	March	April	May	June
A.....	1,427				13,585			
B.....	1,544	1,527			13,346	13,514		
C.....	1,385	1,501	1,585		13,895	13,792	13,835	
D.....	1,622	1,621	1,906	2,057	13,465	13,537	13,430	13,451
E.....		1,499	1,586	1,801		13,796	13,686	13,715
F.....			1,885	2,037			13,352	13,551
G.....				1,851				13,597
Total....	5,978	6,148	6,962	7,746	54,291	54,639	54,303	54,314

should be made to discover other possible peculiarities of this type of estimate and if any are found to correct them. The advantages of the composite estimating procedure for employment appear to be substantial, especially in the case of month-to-month change. Some advantage will also result from their use with the present system of rotation for estimates of year-to-year change.

The advisability of applying the composite method of estimation to various categories in the labor force reports, such as major industry and occupational groups, class of worker, and the subdivisions of the major categories by age and sex, would seem to follow from the evidence of its usefulness for employment. However, for these and particularly for the other more difficult classifications such as "not at work but with a job," "unpaid family workers," "unable to work," and the hours worked, there may be biases similar to those that affect the reporting of unemployment. If such biases exist and are sufficiently large, they may more than offset the gains in accuracy that the composite method can provide. It is important to study what the effect of the composite method is for such categories. This problem should be part of the long run research program. In addition, information about biases should be accumulated from such partial tests as are possible in the course of the regular operations.

The revision of the concepts and classifications that are used in the survey may affect the extent and seriousness of the biases that have been discussed above. Improvement in interviewing methods may also diminish their importance. The least that can be done, however, is to make available to the statistical profession and other interested users of the survey the best information obtainable on the nature and magnitude of these tendencies so that they can make due allowance for this factor in their use of the figures.

The effect of the differences in the information obtained from households for the first month and for succeeding months can be corrected only by a determination of the amount of bias in each month of experience in being interviewed. If it can be assumed that the bias averages out close to zero for the entire period during which a given set of households is in the sample, and this is a dubious assumption, then the effect of the interview experience can be balanced out by using the succeeding month as well as the preceding month to calculate a composite estimate similar in type to the kind now used. This would involve delay and would be suitable only for the revision of the initial estimates that are prepared each month. It could be used as a device to get at the determination of the magnitude of the effect since the difference between the estimates it produces and those that come from the present composite procedure would be due to the effect of interview experience plus some amount of sampling error. This kind of estimate can be extended to include more months preceding and following the month for which the estimate is prepared. It would provide estimates of the level of employment and unemployment that are more accurate than those that are obtained more promptly by the present procedure. Because of the delay, these estimates would find their usefulness more in the field of economic research and long range studies than in the field of immediate action but their usefulness for administrative decisions should not be underrated.

The effect of repeated interviewing of the same persons or households has been recognized and studied in market research and opinion polling. Respondents tend to observe or recall information more readily about items on which they previously have been questioned. This occurs in labor force surveys, too. A housewife who is asked how many hours her husband worked may discuss the question with her husband after the interview and be better prepared to answer it accurately the following month. However, there may be other effects that are even more important in labor force surveys. Reluctance to report the loss of a job may diminish or increase as the respondent and interviewer become better acquainted. The interviewer may be less inclined to do a thorough job of questioning after she learns the labor force status of the household members in the first interview; and the respondent may be impatient with questions about matters that she reported in the preceding month. The use of telephone interviewing is much less frequent in the first interview than in subsequent interviews, and it may contribute to the effect of reinterviewing. If these aspects of the problem can be studied in connection with other surveys, especially those of government agencies, some additional light may be cast on the problem. In like manner, the studies that the Census Bureau should make will be of value in connection with surveys that are conducted by other agencies. Here is a problem that should be investigated in other major surveys that are conducted by government agencies for the guidance of administrators and the public.

BIBLIOGRAPHY

Bureau of the Census publications and documents:

Subcommittee on Sampling Techniques, A Revised Sample for Current Surveys, December 1942 (revised February 1943)

Labor Force Memoranda, 1 to 5

Enumerators' Instructions for Filling Schedule SS-370f, Monthly Report on the Labor Force, July 1945

Current Population Survey, Supervisor's Manual for Sampling Special Dwelling Places (P-1457a), January 1950

Current Population Survey, How to List (P-2210), September 1950

Current Population Survey, District Supervisor's Manual of Sampling Instructions (P-2240), August 1951

Current Population Survey, Enumerator's Manual, How to List and Enumerate (P-2450), November 1953

Other publications:

Bancroft, Gertrude and Welch, Emmett H., "Recent Experience with Problems of Labor Force Measurement," Journal of the American Statistical Association 41 (1946) 303

Ducoff, Louis J. and Hagood, Margaret J., "Objectives, Uses and Types of Labor Force Data in Relation to Economic Policy," Journal of the American Statistical Association 41 (1946) 293

Ducoff, Louis J. and Hagood, Margaret J., Labor Force Definition and Measurement, Social Science Research Council, 1947

Eckler, A. Ross, "The Revised Census Series of Current Employment Estimates," Journal of the American Statistical Association 40 (1945) 187

Other publications--Continued:

Frankel, Lester R. and Stock, J. Stevens, "On the Sample Survey of Unemployment," Journal of the American Statistical Association 37 (1942) 77

Garabarino, Joseph W., "The Unemployed Worker during a Period of 'Full' Employment," Reprint 50, Institute of Industrial Relations, University of California, 1954

Hansen, Morris H., Hurwitz, William N., and Madow, William G., Sample Survey Methods and Theory, Volume 1, John Wiley & Sons, Inc., 1953

Hauser, Philip M., "The Labor Force and Gainful Workers--Concept, Measurement and Comparability," American Journal of Sociology 54 (1949) 4

Hauser, Philip M. and Pearl, Robert B., "Who are the Unemployed?" Journal of the American Statistical Association 45 (1950) 479

Intensive Review Committee, Appraisal of Census Programs (Report to the Secretary of Commerce), February 1954

International Labour Office, Employment, Unemployment and Labour Force Statistics, a Study of Methods, Geneva, 1948

Jaffe, A. J., "The Application of Attitude Research Methodology toward the Problem of Measuring the Size of the Labor Force," International Journal of Opinion and Attitude Research 1 (1947) 4

Jaffe, A. J. and Stewart, Charles D., Manpower Resources and Utilization: Principles of Working Force Analysis, John Wiley and Sons, Inc., 1951

Long, Clarence D., "The Concept of Unemployment," Quarterly Journal of Economics 57 (1942) 1

Marks, Eli and Mauldin, W. Parker, "Response Errors in Census Research," Journal of the American Statistical Association 45 (1950) 424

Other publications--Continued:

Myers, Howard B. and Webb, John N., "Another Census of Unemployment?" American Journal of Sociology 62 (1937) 521

Organization for European Economic Co-operation, Labour Force Statistics: Sample Survey Methods (Technical Assistance Mission No. 105), 1954

Palmer, Gladys L., "Factors in the Variability of Response in Enumerative Studies," Journal of the American Statistical Association 38 (1943) 143

Review of Economic Statistics, February 1950, series of articles on "How Much Unemployment?"

United Nations, The Labour Force: Problems of Census Definition and Enumeration (Studies of Census Methods, No. 4), 1948

Webbink, Paul (ed.), Labor Mobility and Economic Opportunities, John Wiley & Sons, Inc., 1954